BOOKS BY GEORGE GILDER

THE LARGER AGENDA SERIES

BY **GEORGE GILDER**

WHITTLE DIRECT BOOKS

Photographs: RCA television set, Henry Groskinsky, *Life* magazine ©Time Inc., page 8; silica fiber, L. Keenan Assoc./Image Bank, page 24; QuoTrek machine provided by Data Broadcasting Corporation, page 47; Thomas Lipscomb and Peter Sprague by Rex Rystedt, page 48; Niccoló Machiavelli, The Bettmann Archive, page 50; Richard Snelling by Rex Rystedt, page 56; Claude Shannon, courtesy of the MIT Museum, page 57; William McGowan by Bret Littlehales, page 65; Judge Harold Greene by Katherine Lambert, page 66.

Illustrations by Kurt Vargo

Library of Congress Catalog Card Number: 90-70001
Gilder, George
Life After Television
ISBN 0-9624745-2-5
ISSN 1046-364X

The Larger Agenda Series

The Larger Agenda Series presents original short books by distinguished authors on subjects of importance to managers and policymakers in business and the public sector.

The series is edited and published by Whittle Communications L.P., an independent publishing company. A new book appears approximately every other month. The series reflects a broad spectrum of responsible opinions. In each book the opinions expressed are those of the author, not the publisher or the advertiser.

I welcome your comments on this unique endeavor.

William S. Rukeyser
Editor in Chief

CONTENTS

12:15 AM, Memphis, Tennessee. Packages sorted at main hub.

In the early '70s, Federal Express pioneered overnight air express in the U.S. Today, Federal Express offers reliable air express delivery worldwide.

INTRODUCTION

NEW HOPE FOR THE HARES

As the 1980s roared and tumbled to a close, sirens wailed and moods darkened in Japanese-American relations. Rancorous voices rang out across the Pacific, assailing laziness, greed, and waste in U.S. industry and unfair, even predatory, trade practices in Tokyo. For the first time since World War II, the underpinnings of friendship and prosperity between the U.S. and Asia appeared to be in serious jeopardy.

At the center of the wrangle was an array of strategic technologies, from microchips to advanced televisions, that seemed to promise 21st-century Japan the kind of global supremacy that steam and steel had given 19th-century Britain. Beginning in obscure academic tomes, technological research papers, and Delphic Pentagon documents, the alarms sounded in newspaper headlines and on the covers of newsmagazines, in bestsellers and the broadcast media. They chimed sonorously from the lips of business prophets, scientific pundits, and academic economists. They echoed in classrooms and conference centers from MIT to Berkeley, from Chicago to L.A.

A consensus emerged that the U.S. was a graying and gullible nation, slipping into churlish senility, and that Japan was a mercantilist shyster, seizing power by predatory trade. Paranoia ruled on all sides. *Business Week* aroused Japan's worst fears of an Aryan entente by publishing a Harris Survey showing that the American people saw Japan as a greater threat than the U.S.S.R. A prominent Japanese politician fed U.S. phobias by boasting that Japan could overthrow the global military balance merely by selling advanced memory chips to the Soviet Union instead of to the U.S.

All of America's anxieties seemed to converge on Japan's

20-year, multibillion-dollar effort in high-definition television (HDTV). The next generation of television equipment, HDTV could offer a large 3- by 5-foot flat-panel screen that you could hang on the wall like a picture. You might even mistake it for a window, its images would be so true to life. The new television, full of microchips and other advanced electronics, would function like a state-of-the-art video computer that would not only present pictures but reshape and manipulate them as well. With appropriate peripherals, such as color printers and editing systems, HDTV would transform an array of related industries, from still photography and movies to medical diagnostics and missile defense.

Perhaps the most portentous alarm concerning HDTV came from Richard Elkus Jr., a 20-year veteran of U.S.-Japan electronics wars. Now a microchip capital-equipment entrepreneur, two decades ago he had worked at Ampex Corporation while it struggled to introduce the world's first successful consumer videotape recorder. Then he had watched helplessly as Sony and Panasonic captured this American market. Elkus cryptically identified the essence of the Japanese threat: "They [the Japanese] know that when you push a technology far enough it merges with all surrounding technologies, and when you push a market far enough it engulfs all related markets."

HDTV, as Elkus saw it, would engulf the American computer, microchip, appliance, telephone, film, and industrial-equipment technologies and markets. To prevent this disaster, he said, the U.S. must mobilize massively, combining government, industry, labor, and research universities in a national campaign.

Backing Elkus were prestigious leaders of U.S. microchip companies and related businesses. From Andrew Grove, CEO of Intel, to Jerry Pearlman, CEO of Zenith, from the entire leadership of the American Electronics Association to Jack Kuehler, president of IBM, U.S. industrialists bemoaned the new Japanese threat in consumer products.

Politicians also proposed an array of new government programs to answer the HDTV challenge. Almost everyone concurred that the only way for the U.S. to fight back was to imitate the government-guided, mega-corporation strategies of its rival.

In the international technology race, it sometimes seemed as if the Americans were a convention of hares seeking an appropriate response to the tortoise threat. "If only," said one sprightly hare, "we had a big heavy shell to lug around on our backs"; "if only," said another, "we had short scaly legs"; "if only," said a third, "we had little beady green eyes—*then* we could win!"

The great irony was that in this case the hares were not even losing the race. After all, as the 1980s ended, America's productivity level was almost 50 percent higher than Japan's, the country had three times Japan's telecommunications and computer revenues, and its poor lived better, by most economic measures, than did Japan's middle class. Japan's chief unfair advantage was a vastly overvalued yen—an asset inflicted upon the Japanese, against their long resistance, by American mercantilist politicians who strangely imagined they could strengthen the U.S. by debauching the dollar.

Nonetheless, there was some truth on the side of the alarmists. All was not well with American business and culture. America's schools were pathetic compared to Japan's, with the top 1 percent of students scoring below the average Japanese student on international math and science tests. U.S. culture was increasingly dominated by mindless television shows, violent or prurient movies, and nihilistic or absurdist art and literature. Finance was increasingly hostile to technology. Politics was preoccupied with short-term fixes and xenophobic fables.

The American hares certainly will lose if they bound off in panic, chasing illusory technologies and government solutions. American business certainly cannot prevail if it fatally focuses on the competition rather than on its own customers. Yet many U.S. business leaders seem more interested in keeping out Japanese products or collaborating with Japanese projects in consumer electronics than in pursuing the huge promise of America's own information technologies.

Through the research I conducted for my book *Microcosm: The Quantum Revolution in Economics and Technology*, which was published in late 1989, it became clear to me that the new national strategy of imitating Japan was radically misconceived. I had explored the history and nature of microchip technology, showing that its reach and promise were inexorably global. But before I had even completed writing the book, U.S. politicians began advocating a new economic nationalism that defied the very nature of microelectronics as I saw it.

I had written in *Microcosm* that television, in technical terms, was dead. Now, industry leaders are solemnly presenting high-definition television as the new hope of the future. In *Microcosm*, I had shown that the freedom and creativity of the American entrepreneurial system had given the U.S. the lead over Japan in many of the most critical computer technologies. Now the U.S. is engaging in a passionate siege of self-abuse, with experts advocating that America create new government bureaucracies and business consortia to catch up with Japan.

In this book, moving beyond the physical laws underlying microchip technology, I will show that the microchip will reshape not only the television and computer industries but also the telecommunications industry and all other information services. It will transform business, education, and art. It can renew our entire culture. The downfall of television turns out to be only the most visible symbol of a series of cascading changes that will engulf the world in the 1990s.

Large organizations, from broadcasting networks to government bureaucracies, from multinational corporate hierarchies to centralized school systems, are in jeopardy. But what will replace them? If the U.S. can still prevail in the central technologies of the age, what strategies should its companies and politicians pursue?

New governmental policies are imperative. The U.S. will have to adopt a genuinely new strategy in the technology race, moving entirely beyond television into a realm of new technology. Rather than playing a sure losing game of catch-up-and-copy with Japan, America will have to fulfill the creative promise of its own systems and technologies.

Despite a number of defeats and frustrations, there is still hope for the hares. But they will have to understand that their problems started at home and that the solutions will be found there, too.

The U.S. can maintain world industrial leadership, not by focusing on the strengths and foibles of Japan, but by tapping its own unique resources and treating its many self-inflicted wounds. Rather than imitating Japanese television technology, America can exploit its own globally dominant computer and telecommunications industries. A crucial step will be to overthrow the legal and regulatory structures that have prevented America's most powerful companies from leading the world to "life after television." But to achieve this new goal, the U.S. will first have to understand why television has for so long dominated the world's entertainment and culture, and why it has now become obsolete.

3:36 PM, Geneva, Switzerland. Overseas shipment delivered to its final destination.

With 30 million international express deliveries under our belt,
Federal Express provides unmatched expertise in dutiable
and document shipments overseas.

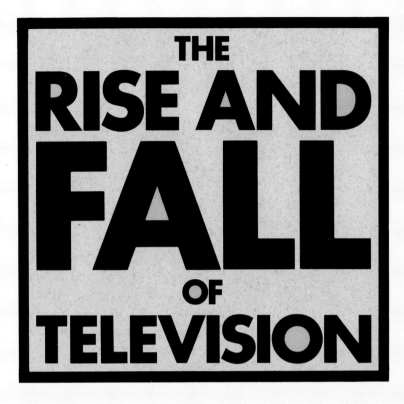

THE RISE AND FALL OF TELEVISION

At the 1939 World's Fair, the American people got their first glimpse of a device that would launch a new era of popular culture. Enshrined at the center of the RCA exhibit was a large contraption composed mainly of vacuum tubes in a box with a small screen attached. Like most new technologies, it aped the old, resembling an oversized radio with a gray window on the front. Although many observers sensed the power of this amazing new machine for video communications, few of them grasped anything about its coming impact on American culture and society. Most people could not have anticipated that this glowing Cyclops would give its name to a new age: the age of television.

Even after World War II, when the networks emerged with their small following of local affiliates, few people understood the profound changes that television would bring. Offering a snowy flicker of black-and-white images and relatively few programs or advertisements, TV seemed to be a futuristic technology many years away from making a major impact. "Nobody in radio wanted to have anything to do with us,"

RCA launched the TV era by introducing the first set at the 1939 World's Fair.

said Art Lodge, an NBC–TV newswriter in 1950. Radio was still the utterly dominant broadcast medium, filling the nation's homes with music, news, and entertainment. Radio's champions had little interest in promoting a potential usurper.

Few people could imagine that in a decade or so television would become a peremptory force in American culture, defining the news, reshaping politics, reorienting family life, and remaking the cultural expectations of several generations of Americans. No one predicted that in a few decades 98 percent of all American households would own a television set, exceeding the level of telephone ownership by five percentage points, and by a far larger margin in the homes of the poor. No one anticipated that the members of an average household would watch the screen some six hours a day, while in poor homes television would become a substitute hearth, glowing constantly day and night. Few people foresaw that television, more than any other force, would provide the unifying images that would define the national experience and consciousness.

Television marched into America's living rooms and took over for 50 years. First it transformed childhood into Howdy Doody time, adolescence into puberty rites with Elvis Presley and the Beatles, and politics into news bites on the networks. Television took us to Little Rock, Arkansas, and Birmingham, Alabama, blessing the civil rights movement for two decades. It cast infamy on Orval Faubus and Bull Connor and beatified Martin Luther King, contributing heavily to the passage of new laws against discrimination. For three decades television exalted feminism and other forms of sexual liberation. TV took us to Dallas and made John F. Kennedy into a national icon. It took us to the moon. It awakened us to the horrors of war in Vietnam. It made a few hundred corpses on Beijing's Tiananmen Square loom larger in the American mind than the many millions of deaths that occurred under the rule of Chairman Mao Tse-tung.

Television heavily determined which books and magazines we read, which cultural figures ascended to celebrity and wealth, and which politicians prospered or collapsed. It pilloried Joseph McCarthy, Lyndon Johnson, and Richard

Nixon. It made Ronald Reagan the most popular president of the era.

Like any domineering ruler, television made mistakes. But it contributed more to the U.S. standard of living than any other single invention. It received a readier welcome in households than the cheaper telephone because it offered a better yield for the money. In terms of access to news and entertainment, television made the poorest of American families far richer than kings and tycoons of old.

The television age is giving way to the much richer, interactive technologies of the computer age.

By all measures, TV was a superb technology for its time. Indeed, its presence and properties defined the time. But now its time is over. The television age is giving way to the much richer, interactive technologies of the computer age.

The overthrow of television was already assured at the moment of its initial triumph. Television is a broadcast medium shaped by the characteristics of the vacuum tube and the radio-frequency spectrum. As these technologies were beset by more powerful rivals, the future of television fell into jeopardy. To fully understand why the original technologies were so rapidly outmoded, we must first understand the basic science behind them.

For decades, television systems operated mainly through the use of vacuum tubes, which are sealed and evacuated glass cylinders. These tubes translate sound and the lights of an image into powerful waves that can radiate through the air from a broadcasting station and be detected by TV antennas miles away. The tubes were used to magnify and process these waves for display on a phosphorescent screen, which is itself a very large vacuum tube. Indeed, at every point in a television system where weak or blurry signals need to be enhanced, refined, or amplified, the vacuum tube came into play.

A key constraint in television technology lies in the flow of signals through the air. Sending the signals requires the use of a portion of the electromagnetic spectrum called radio frequencies, which are highly vulnerable to interference in the atmosphere.

The electromagnetic spectrum is composed of electrical charges that produce magnetism, which in turn generates electricity in a perpetual spiral through the air. This electromagnetic wave action, modulated by picture signals, makes long-distance TV transmission possible.

Waves in the spectrum crest like waves in the ocean. The distance from crest to crest is the wavelength. The number of waves, or vibrations, per second is the frequency. These vibrations per second, which are called hertz, carry the sound, color, and brightness information required for the television-broadcasting system. The number of hertz that can be transmitted across a particular medium is called its bandwidth.

The human ear can detect frequencies between 30 and 20,000 hertz. These very low frequencies are called sounds. The human eye can detect wavelengths between 400 and 700 nanometers (billionths of a meter) or frequencies around 10 to the 20th power. These relatively high frequencies are called colors. Sound and color frequencies cannot be broadcast long distances for use in television. They must be translated into the radio-frequency portion of the electromagnetic spectrum. These frequencies, capable of being sent long distances, occupy parts of the spectrum between the waves of sound and color.

Because higher and lower frequencies tend to be lost in the atmosphere over long distances, only frequencies between hundreds of thousands and millions of hertz (kilohertz and megahertz) can carry ground-based radio and television signals. These frequencies reside in what we call "the air," which is usable for radio and television broadcasting, cellular phones, air phones, pagers, and other mobile technologies. Higher frequencies, with billions of waves per second (gigahertz), can be used for direct-broadcast satellite transmission.

All of these frequencies combined constitute the radio-frequency spectrum, or simply "the spectrum." Television stations modulate and transmit these frequencies in the form of powerful waves reverberating forth in circles from an electrically charged antenna. Each television station in the U.S. usually requires exclusive use of the six megahertz needed to bear a television signal. Because of interference, however, each station also must have unoccupied spectrum space surrounding the signal. This insulating space is several times larger than the signal itself. In all, television occupies about 40 percent of the spectrum. The spectrum is a scarce resource because in any locality only a limited number of frequencies are available to transmit information.

The nature of both the vacuum tube and the radio-frequency spectrum shaped the powers and limitations of television as an information medium and a cultural force. These technologies dictated that television would be a top-down system—in electronic terms, a "master-slave" architecture. A few broadcast centers would originate programs for millions of passive receivers, or "dumb terminals."

The expense and complexity of the tubes used in television systems meant that most of the processing of signals would have to be done at the station. The TV had to be relatively simple, because designers had to keep costs down by using the lowest possible number of vacuum tubes in the sets. Storage of signals was out of the question, since a memory might require millions of vacuum tubes in a single set.

Television easily triumphed over its technical flaws, and the world came to see it as a fact of life. TV was "the air."

With little storage or processing possible at the set, the signals transmitted by broadcasting stations would have to be directly displayable waves, resembling as closely as possible the sounds and images to be presented. This meant that TV would have to be an analog system, since analog waves directly simulate sound, brightness, and color.

The advantage of analog systems is efficiency; the entire wave is used to carry, imitate, and display the signal. The disadvantages are sensitivity to atmospheric interference and difficulty of manipulation and storage. Because the entire analog wave is used to carry information, any distortion of the wave results in distortion of the picture.

Economic and technical constraints pushed the critical electronics out of the TV set and back into the broadcasting station. Nearly all of the system's intelligence—shaping, sequencing, and storing picture signals—would have to be located at the broadcasting center.

The television set was the bottleneck. Its processing power would limit the form of the signals used, the resolution of the picture, and the number of channels. The processing power of the box—its bandwidth—was minute compared with the processing power at the station.

Yet television easily triumphed over its technical flaws, and the world came to see it as a fact of life. TV was "the air." Several inventions, however, ultimately dislodged the key props of the television age. The invention of the transistor in 1948, the microchip in 1958, and the fiber-optic cable in the late 1970s made the top-down broadcast structure, with most of the intelligence at the station, obsolete.

Transistors, which are simple and cheap devices made from

the silicon in sand, could perform nearly all the amplifying functions of the tubes except for actually displaying the picture. The integrated circuit, or microchip, gave the world the capability to combine many transistors on one tiny piece of silicon. Perhaps sensing the deadly long-run implications the microchip would have for the medium, the U.S. television industry at first resisted these innovations. In 1966 advertisements, Zenith actually boasted of its "hand-crafted" quality with "no plastic printed circuit boards, no production short-cuts. Every connection is carefully hand-wired." The Japanese adopted the new microchip devices first and used them to break into the U.S. market with cheaper and incomparably more durable sets.

Microchips served initially as cheap substitutes for the vacuum tube. As the years passed, however, the microchip industry spawned an unending series of innovations that would doom all top-down broadcasting systems. With millions—yes, millions— of vacuum-tube equivalents printed on single slivers of silicon costing less than one dollar to make, cheap video receivers in the 1990s would no longer have to be dumb or dependent on distant stations for processing power.

Far from a stripped-down box with nothing in it but a few vacuum tubes and copper wires, the set could become a personal computer, a powerful processor with millions or even billions of tube equivalents that could perform functions well beyond mere display. It could create, perfect, process, store, and even transmit signals on its own. Although microchips first were used to extend the life of ordinary receivers and videocassette recorders, eventually they would radically change the very nature of the medium.

Intelligence could move from the broadcast station into inexpensive home-based personal computers. The PC would eventually be able to manipulate video signals at the user's will, zooming in and out, performing replays, storing and even editing pictures. This video-processing power at the set would greatly reduce the need for complex and costly equipment at the event to be broadcast or at the broadcast station. A concert could be taped, for example, with just four video cameras, and then transmitted to give the viewer a 360-degree image that he could shape at the PC. The choices now made by broadcasters at the event could be made at home by a viewer's hand-held remote control.

The advent of microchip technology was well timed, because even the air began to give out. With the rapid spread of mobile technologies led by the nearly ubiquitous cellular phones, the air became a valuable and limited resource. The Motorola-Timex wristwatch pager, which displays the number and identity of the caller, portends an ultimate vision of the wristwatch telephone, with everyone using spectrum for personal communication.

TV broadcasters have been the world's biggest air hogs. With no alternative technology in sight and few competing uses for the air, however, television has not until now had to justify its immense demands for spectrum. But in the 1980s, just as the microchip had transformed the dimensions of electronics, fiber optics reshaped the possibilities of all media. The limitations of the air, and even of the coaxial copper wires that carry cable television, gave way to the unlimited bandwidth of lasers and glass. Fiber-optic glass wires the width of a human hair could potentially bear billions or even trillions of characters of information per second.

These data were digital in form, which meant that all the information for sound, brightness, and color was numerically encoded. Digital signals have an advantage over analog signals in that they can be stored and manipulated without deteriorating. These signals could potentially be switched through two-way telephone networks, collected on new kinds of memories resembling compact discs, and processed and displayed by personal computers. A huge variety of programs could be dispatched over fiber lines. A small box of disks by the desk could hold whole libraries of pay-per-view video entertainment, art, and information. High-quality, full-motion video no longer needed to be broadcast through the air or through copper cables.

No longer was there any justification for allowing television to hog the spectrum. No longer was there any reason

12:10 AM, Memphis, Tennessee. Shipments loaded at sort facility.

With the largest all-cargo air fleet in the world, Federal Express provides air express delivery to all major international markets.

9:23 AM, Bruges, Belgium. Overseas delivery.

Sending a package overseas? Federal Express has over
28,000 couriers worldwide who can deliver. On time.

for video to use a vulnerable, complex, inefficient, and unmanipulable signal. No longer was there any logic in leaving the brains of the system at the station. The age of television, for all intents and purposes, was over.

Like all technologies superseded by more powerful inventions, television would not readily disappear. The corpse would remain in American living rooms for many more years. But the fate of technologies is defined not by their prevalence but by their competitiveness and promise. By that measure, the mostly analog "idiot box" and videocassette tape player were as passé as last century's icebox and ice wagon.

The new system will be the telecomputer, a personal computer adapted for video processing and connected by fiber-optic threads to other telecomputers all around the world. Using a two-way system of signals like telephones do, rather than broadcasting one-way like TV, the telecomputer will surpass the television in video communication just as the telephone surpassed the telegraph in verbal communication.

Today, in feasibility, quality, and speed of advance, this new system promises far more than television did in 1950. Computer technology, dominated by the microchip, approximately doubles in power every year. As its power rises, its price declines and its market increases. Within a span of about seven years, any computer function will drop to one-tenth the current cost or grow 10 times in power. Largely because of price reductions, the number of personal computers in offices rose more than tenfold in just the six years from 1981 to 1987. Use in homes rose more than twentyfold. Some 40 million personal computers—half the world's total number of PCs—now reside in U.S. worksites and homes.

In presenting one-way news and entertainment, telecomputers can already do anything that present-day televisions can do. But they will soon offer a plethora of new computer functions. Telecomputers have interactive powers, from voice-controlled video to image creation and retrieval, that are inherently impossible in an analog broadcast medium.

The telecomputer's impact on every facet of American life

and culture will be fully as potent as the impact of television has been. But the telecomputer's influence will be radically different. The telecomputer may even reverse the effects of the television age.

Rather than exalting mass culture, the telecomputer will enhance individualism. Rather than cultivating passivity, the telecomputer will promote creativity. Instead of a master-slave architecture, the telecomputer will have an interactive architecture in which every receiver can function as a processor and transmitter of video images and other information. The telecomputer will usher in a new culture compatible with the immense powers of today's ascendant technology.

Perhaps most important, the telecomputer will enrich and strengthen democracy and capitalism all around the world. The television industry is currently congratulating itself for the role Western programs have played in promoting the overthrow of communist regimes in Eastern Europe. This claim is largely true. Yet television is at its heart a totalitarian medium. Because television signals originate at a single station and are sent top-down to the masses, tyrants everywhere push TV sets onto their people.

Thus, the U.S.S.R. has 306 television sets for every 1,000 people—a ratio nearly as high as in Western Europe. But the Soviets have only one-third as many telephones as TVs and only one computer for every 306 TVs. The U.S. and other democracies have a high ratio of telephones and computers to people. West Germany, for example, has almost six times as many phones per capita as the Soviet Union but only one-fifth more TVs. These ratios are changing as communist countries allow their people more freedom, and they constitute a good index of democratization in those countries.

The top-down television system is an alien and corrosive force in democratic capitalism. Contrary to the rich and variegated promise of new technology proliferating options on every hand, TV squeezes the consciousness of an entire nation through a few score channels.

Increasingly, it is shaping the consciousness of the entire world. American mass entertainment is the most powerful force in global culture. Its appeal is so seductive that broadcasting regulators around the world are restricting the number of American programs on their airwaves. This practice is in part a simple show of protectionism, but it also reflects the attitude that a country dominated by U.S. television has been invaded as surely as if by military imperialists.

Full-motion video and high-fidelity audio are by far the most powerful media tools ever invented by man. They simply overwhelm all other media. But to use them today, the artist usually has to make a Faustian deal. He must give up his individuality and creativity. He must bow to the lowest terms of mass appeal. Then he must join the queue for access to the limited number of video-entertainment channels. Television acts as a severe bottleneck to creative expression, driving thousands of American writers and creators into formulaic banality or near-pornographic pandering.

The current system dictates that thousands of writers and directors labor to supply a few channels and distributors and that few of America's best TV and motion picture artists regularly have their work produced. Rather than creating original works, most TV writers merely fill in the blanks of formatted shows, contriving shocks and sensations to satisfy a mass audience. The entertainment industry pays them well, not to create innovative programming, but to endlessly work and rework a few proven themes.

On the fringes of the television and film industries, however, American creativity is beginning to burst forth through VCRs, cable, low-power channels, public-television programs, low-budget movies, and a huge variety of new computer software. In text, where the impact of digital technology came first and most fully, desktop-publishing programs have generated tens of thousands of new publishing ventures such as special-interest magazines. These developments offer the merest glimpse of the possibilities of digital video. Released from the restrictions of mass media, American culture could attain new levels in both the visual arts and literature.

The very nature of broadcasting, however, means that television cannot cater to the special interests of audiences dispersed across the country. Television is not vulgar because people are vulgar; it is vulgar because people are similar in

Television acts as a severe bottleneck to creative expression, driving thousands of American writers and creators into formulaic banality.

their prurient interests and sharply differentiated in their civilized concerns. All of world industry is moving increasingly toward more segmented markets. But in a broadcast medium, such a move would be a commercial disaster. In a broadcast medium, artists and writers cannot appeal to the highest aspirations and sensibilities of individuals. Instead, manipulative masters rule over huge masses of people.

Television is a tool of tyrants. Its overthrow will be a major force for freedom and individuality, culture and morality. That overthrow is at hand.

3:52 PM, Minneapolis, Minnesota. Message relayed.

With COSMOS® our advanced satellite-based communication system,
the status of your package is just a phone call away.

4:42 PM, London, England. The SuperTracker encodes package information.

To verify the location of your packages, the Federal Express SuperTracker®
enters the data into our computerized COSMOS® tracking system.

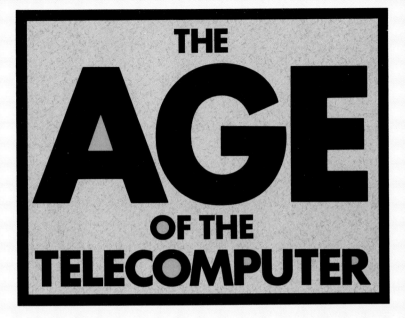

THE AGE OF THE TELECOMPUTER

Let us contemplate a vision of sand. In legend and scripture, sand often serves as a symbol of frivolity and impermanence. In this vision, however, it serves as the foundation for a new world economy that will last through the next century.

Sand in the form of crystalline silicon is used in microelectronics, which is based on switching electrons through the infinitesimal circuitry of computers. Sand in the form of silica fibers is used in photonics, the technology of transmitting and switching light through strands of glass, or fiber-optic cables.

In microelectronics, the crystalline silicon is sliced into tiny slivers about a quarter-inch square, each imprinted with a microscopic maze of switches and wires. The switches are transistors and the wires interconnect them. Each interconnection is called a node. As the maze becomes more dense, with millions of tiny devices concentrated on a single microchip, it will enable telecomputers to summon and shape images with resolution far exceeding current film technology or future high-definition television.

The glass of the silica fibers used in photonics is so pure that you could see through miles of it as easily as through a windowpane. It is manufactured in threads thinner than a human hair and longer than Long Island. Bearing tiny pulses of light across continents and under seas, these strands of glass can transmit quantities of information many thousands of times more voluminous than what large copper cables or satellites can carry today.

At present, microchips and fiber optics are the world's most rapidly advancing technologies. Separately, these technologies will have a large impact on our future. Together, they will create a new system that can transform the possibilities of all human society.

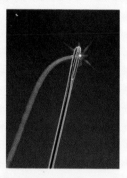

The silica fibers used in fiber-optic cables are manufactured in threads thinner than a hair and longer than Long Island.

Tired of watching TV? With artful programming of telecomputers, you could spend a day interacting on the screen with Henry Kissinger, Kim Basinger, or Billy Graham. Celebrities could produce and sell their own software or make themselves available for two-way personal video communication. You could take a fully interactive course in physics or computer science with the world's most exciting professors, who respond to your questions and let you move at your own learning speed. You could have a fully interactive workday without commuting to the office or run a global corporation without ever getting on a plane.

You could watch your child play baseball at a high school across the county, view the Super Bowl from any point in the stadium that you choose, or soar above the basket with Michael Jordan. You could fly an airplane over the Alps or climb Mount Everest—all on a powerful high-resolution display.

The possibilities are endless: Create a school in your home that offers the nation's best teachers imparting the moral, cultural, and religious values you cherish. Visit your family on the other side of the world with moving pictures hardly distinguishable from real-life images. Have your doctor make house calls without leaving his office. Give a birthday party for Grandma at her nursing home in Florida, bringing her descendants from all over the country to the foot of her bed in vivid living color. Watch movies or television programs originating from any station or digital database in the world reachable by telephone lines. Order and instantly receive magazines, books, or other publications from almost anywhere in the world, edited to your own taste. You could potentially call up any of these functions, and unlimited others, through listings on a telecomputer menu or in new magazines.

All of these telecomputer functions are possible today through the alchemy of sand and glass in computer and fiber-optic technology. These technologies can fall into the financial reach of most Americans within a decade or so, since their cost-effectiveness is doubling nearly every year. A crystalline web of glass and light, manufactured and installed by American businesses and workers, will soon stretch across the U.S.

Through this crystal web, we can reclaim our culture from the centralized influence of mass media. We can liberate our imaginations from programs regulated by bureaucrats, chosen by a small elite of broadcasting professionals, and governed by the need to target the lowest common denominators of public interests.

To fulfill the promise of this technology, however, we must define our goals and then resourcefully seek them. Technology is not a genie in a bottle or an overwhelming tide engulfing us from afar. It is not something that happens to us inexorably and chaotically like a Tolstoyan war. It is something we create or suppress largely as we see fit.

From the personal computer to the fiber-optic cable, from the communications satellite to the compact disc, our generation commands the most powerful information tools in history. Yet the culture we have created with these machines is dreary at best. Why doesn't our superb information technology better inform and uplift us?

This is the most important question of the age. The most dangerous threat to the U.S. economy and society is the breakdown of our cultural institutions—in the family, religion, education, and the arts—that preserve and transmit civilization to new generations. If this social fabric continues to fray, we will lose not only our technological prowess and economic competitiveness but also the meaning of life itself. The chief economic challenge we now face is how to apply the new technologies in a way that preserves the values and disciplines that made them possible in the first place.

Conventional economics has little to say about such issues.

Focusing on mathematical and quantitative images of the economy, economists usually treat technological progress and moral values as exogenous: forces outside the system. But these "outside" forces can overwhelm anything measured by the economists.

No fiscal or monetary policy, however brilliant, will be able to promote enduring economic growth and competitiveness in a society in which children spend four hours a day wallowing in the nihilistic swamp of television. Families and schools cannot succeed unless our culture upholds moral codes and disciplines and hard regimens of study. In the U.S., culture means TV. It means an endless flow of minor titillations with barely a major idea or ideal. The culture propagated by TV and other media is perhaps economically exogenous, but it is central to what happens to the economy.

Information technology is the defining activity of modern man and American society.

In 1969, Alan Kiron, a staff scientist at the U.S. Patent Office, coined the term *domonetics* to describe the interactions between culture and technology. Combining the words *domicile*, *connections*, and *electronics*, Kiron used the term to describe how work and living patterns would be reshaped by the new computer and other communications tools. The concept of domonetics was filed away and forgotten. With the rapid emergence of microchip and fiber-optic technology, its resurrection is now imperative.

Domonetics focuses on flows of communication. Rather than identifying hierarchies, counting units, and defining boundaries—as economics does—domonetics stresses social and technological connections. While economists speak in the language of mechanics, leverage, and equilibrium, domonetics is best described through neural metaphors. From telephones and televisions to computers and telecomputers—linked by wires and switches, fields and forces—information technology is the central nervous system of the domonetic world. It is the defining activity of modern man and American society. We live inside our televisions, computers, and telephones as much as we live inside our homes.

The most prestigious universities and most learned scientists are trying to plan an orderly passage to this domonetic world. The most visionary bureaucracies, from IBM, AT&T,

and the Defense Advanced Research Projects Agency (DARPA) in the U.S. to Japan's NTT, NEC, and the Ministry of International Trade and Industry (MITI), are trying to determine how to profit from it. Media giants are trying to find synergy in some new shuffle of computers, broadcasting facilities, optical disks, videocassettes, microchips, and magazines. Despite all of these efforts, the technologies that determine our lifestyles too often go awry. The phone system has become a maze of options that customers often don't want or need; the television system is an even vaster wasteland than it was in the time of Newton Minow. The computer still has kinks, and the software is years behind the times. Movie theaters multiply to show films scarcely more varied or savory than their overpriced candy and soda.

Yes, there is a computer in the kitchen and under the hood and on every other desk. But wherever the U.S. economy has most readily embraced these new "productivity tools," experts in both government and industry can find hardly any new growth of productivity.

The turbid stream of failed prophecies, flubbed projects, and unexpected outcomes reflects a profound misunderstanding of the information tools at the very heart of all of these industries, from consumer electronics to telecommunications. The central nervous system will continue to twitch spastically, in embarrassing ways, as long as bureaucrats and politicians fail to comprehend the nature and promise of this new technology. The U.S. will not compete successfully with Asia in these domains if the established powers persistently misunderstand and suppress the most promising new developments.

Microchips, telephones, mainframe computers, and television systems are all networks of wires and switches. Therefore, they are all governed on one level by the simple but compelling laws that rule all such network systems. By comprehending the powerful forces that have been shaping the microelectronics of networks for the past decade, we can understand the errors of the past, the discomfiture of the experts, and the likely fate of heralded technologies such as high-definition television.

The domonetics of current systems can be summed up in one key principle. In all networks of wires and switches, except for those on the microchip, complexity tends to grow exponentially as the number of interconnections rises. This rule applies to national computer networks, to telephone connections, even to interactions in a national economic plan. In all such cases, the multiplication of interconnections and switches rapidly reaches a level of exploding complexity that the human mind, even aided by computers, is unable to reduce to a manageable order.

Arno Penzias, the Nobel laureate research vice-president of AT&T Bell Laboratories, offers the analogy of an additional child arriving at a party. With one more child the level of noise does not rise arithmetically in proportion to the addition of another set of vocal cords. Rather, the rise in racket usually reflects the number of possible interactions between the extra child and all the other children at the party. Similarly, when one child leaves, the noise level drops not by simple subtraction but by the reduction in the number of possible interactions between that child and all the others.

This phenomenon of exponentially growing complexity could be called the law of the macrocosm. In Newtonian physics, it is often called the many-body problem. While computing the interactions between a small number of planets or other physical entities is feasible, computing a large number causes what is called a combinatorial explosion.

In the silicon mazes of microchip technology, however, a radically different rule applies. This is the law of the microcosm. The microcosm is the domain of the infinitesimal, of atomic phenomena ruled by the principles of quantum physics. Comprehensible only through quantum physics and far too small for human beings to see directly or control, transistor networks inscribed on individual microchips transcend the law of exponentially growing complexity.

The law of the microcosm is nearly the converse of the law of the macrocosm. In the microcosm, efficiency, not complexity, grows as the square of the number of interconnections, or switches, to be organized.

3:28 PM, Somerset, New Jersey. Incoming calls are handled.

Questions about overseas delivery?
Talk to a specially trained international expert toll-free.
24 hours a day. 365 days a year.

10:07 AM, Munich. Courier making deliveries.

When you send your package with Federal Express—
domestic or international—we take care of your shipment
every step of the way.

On the microchip, the smaller and more densely packed the wires and switches, the faster, cheaper, and more reliable the system. Electronics works best when the movements of electrons approach their geodesic—the shortest possible distance they can travel without colliding with the crystalline structure of the silicon. On the microchip, the immense precision and speed of infinitesimal quantum phenomena can countervail the friction, resistance, entropy, and chaotic movement of all visible things.

On the microchip, the more numerous and close together the transistors, the better they work and the more efficient the system. It is as though another million kids arrived at the party and the noise level went down. At present, the smallest controlled movements of electrons on microchips are hundreds of times longer than their geodesic. This leaves huge and perhaps ever-growing room for progress in microelectronics.

Today, for example, some 20 million transistors can be put onto a single sliver of silicon. Within the next 10 years, a single microchip may contain no fewer than a billion transistors— each one a flawlessly operating switch interconnected with tiny wires. It will eventually be possible to manufacture this chip for a few dollars. On networks off a chip, however, interconnecting a billion of anything would cost untold trillions of dollars.

The coming era, therefore, will be one of single microchip systems. More and more processing power will devolve to particular slivers of silicon running individual personal computers. More and more authority will slip from the tops of hierarchies onto the desktops of individual entrepreneurs and engineers.

The force of microelectronics will blow apart all the monopolies, hierarchies, pyramids, and power grids of established industrial society.

The force of microelectronics will blow apart all the monopolies, hierarchies, pyramids, and power grids of established industrial society. It will undermine all totalitarian regimes. Police states cannot endure under the advance of the computer because it increases the powers of the people far faster than the powers of surveillance. All hierarchies will tend to become "heterarchies"—systems in which each individual rules his own domain. In contrast to a hierarchy ruled from the top, a heterarchy is a society of equals under the law.

For the last two decades, the law of the microcosm has been the most potent force in the computer business. In 1977, large computers costing more than $20,000 commanded nearly 100 percent of the world's computer power; in 1987, they commanded less than 1 percent. By 1987, there were 80 million personal computers in the world—half of them in the U.S.—and their collective computing power dwarfed the total of large computers. The geodesic network of transistors on single chips has displaced the complex command center of a giant mainframe computer connected by wires to dumb terminals. The intelligence in the network is no longer concentrated in a powerful computer at the top. The intelligence is distributed throughout the system.

Switches are the source of machine intelligence; wires are the pathways of communication. The plummeting cost of switches in relation to wires collapses the cost of intelligence in relation to interconnection. This means that centralized systems with dumb boxes attached have become outdated. Top-down systems, whether mainframe computers, central telephone switches, broadcasting networks, or local TV stations, are all vulnerable.

A steadily increasing share of video communications is already conducted over computer networks rather than over broadcasting systems. Propelled by relatively low-volume uses such as video teleconferencing or engineering workstations sending complex design drafts, the trend toward interactive architecture remains sluggish. But the meteoric ascent of the fax machine, using digital video images consisting chiefly of text, illustrates the power of this interactive technology. It is the next beckoning frontier of the computer revolution. Digital video is on the verge of an explosive upsurge as fast as the fax's and far more significant. It will eventually sweep through the entire world of broadcasting and consumer electronics. Television, the dumbest box of all, will give way to the telecomputer, or the "teleputer," linked to the world with fiber-optic cables.

In order to connect another device to a television terminal, even a VCR, you first have to transform the message into the intricate analog hieroglyphs of the television code and then modulate it onto a high-frequency carrier as if it were traveling miles through the air. This complex protocol harshly restricts the possibilities for interaction. You cannot talk back to the TV without going through channels. During an age when technology is unleashing an ever-more-varied array of specialized products, the television-broadcasting pyramid is the supreme anachronism.

The new law of networks exalts the smallest coherent system: the individual human mind and spirit. A healthy culture reflects not the psychology of crowds but the creativity and inspiration of millions of individuals reaching for high goals. In place of the broadcast pyramid, a peer network will emerge in which all the terminals will be smart—not mere television sets but interactive video receivers, processors, and transmitters.

The telecomputer could revitalize public education by bringing the best teachers in the country to classrooms everywhere. More important, the telecomputer could encourage competition because it could make home schooling both feasible and attractive. To learn social skills, neighborhood children could gather in micro-schools run by parents, churches, or other local institutions. The competition of home schooling would either destroy the public school system or force it to become competitive with rival systems, including those in Asia that now set the global standard.

Every morning, millions of commuters across America sit in cars inching their way toward cluttered, polluted, and crime-ridden cities. Or they sit in dilapidated trains rattling toward office towers that survive as business centers chiefly because of their superior access to the global network of computers and telecommunications. With telecomputers in every home attached to a global fiber network, why would anyone commute? People would be able to see the boss life-size in high-definition video and meet with him as easily at home as at the office. They would be able to reach with equal immediacy the head of the foreign subsidiary or the marketing chief across the country. They would be able to send and receive documents almost instantly from anywhere. Downtown offices might be filled with clerks, but anyone with executive responsibilities would tend more and more to stay home.

People will always seek the physical and psychological pleasures of traveling. They will still go to Waikiki to lie on the beach, ride the surf, or drink piña coladas with fun-loving playmates. But they could also go comfortably sightseeing from their living rooms through high-resolution screens, visiting third-world countries without having to worry about exchange rates or air fares.

Meanwhile, across the country, impatient viewers sit on their couches in front of TV screens, clicking their remote panels through an array of channels until something catches the eye. Is it lesbian nuns on *Donahue*, a baseball game, a riot in Lebanon, Judge Wapner, a congressman deploring dirty air or deficits, Miss September naked on the beach in Aruba, an aerobic hunk rhythmically stretching, Louis Rukeyser and three market analysts predicting boom and bust—what will it be, folks? Adjusting for sexual preferences, it's a few minutes with Miss September or the aerobic hunk. Then off to the video store, right? But even at the video store, for the same reasons of mass-media economics, there will be the same sort of choices.

All right, let's go to the movies. There are 50 theaters within driving distance, but they are showing only 10 movies. Five of them are for teeny-boppers or perverts. Two are comedies about men and babies. One is about corrupt cops, call girls, and drug runners. You have already seen the other two. Perhaps one was worth the effort. The same requirement of achieving mass appeal that afflicts TV also restricts films to a few vulgar themes or sure-fire sensations.

By radically changing the balance of power between the distributors and creators of culture, the telecomputer will forever break the broadcast bottleneck. Potentially, there will be as many channels as there are computers attached to the global network. The creator of a program on a specialized subject—from fly-fishing to quantum physics—will be able to reach with one video everyone in the United States, Europe, and Asia who shares the interest.

He will be able to command a large audience without worrying about mass appeal. The medium will change from a mass-produced and mass-consumed commodity to an endless feast of niches and specialties.

Today, some 30 percent of the movie dollar goes to distribution. The masters of the bottleneck charge a toll to the queued-up creators seeking to reach the public and a toll to the public seeking the creators' work. In the fiber-optic network, however, the share of the entertainment dollar going to distribution will drop below 5 percent. With essentially unlimited bandwidth, the cost of adding another option on a fiber cable will be negligible. The operators of fiber networks will want above all to fill them with programs. A huge variety of suppliers will gain access to audiences, and money will pass from the distributors to the creators. But this will not be a zero-sum game. The distributors will do better too because of an explosive expansion of the market.

Big events—the Super Bowl or the election debates or the most compelling mass programs—will still command their audiences, which can be reached by direct-broadcast satellite or broadcasts through fiber-optic cables. But all the media junk food and filler that stretches out toward the horizons of mass culture like so much strip development will tend to disappear. People will order what they want rather than settling for what is there. In the world of the telecomputer, broadcasters, educators, investors, and filmmakers, who thought they could never go broke underestimating the intelligence of the American people, are going to discover that they were wrong.

The position of the broadcasters parallels the stance of mass magazines before the rise of television and the proliferation of a thousand specialized magazines. The TV networks are the *Look* and *Life*, the *Collier's* and *Saturday Evening Post*, of the current cultural scene. *Look* and *Collier's* are dead; the *Post* has survived in a much-reduced form by becoming a health magazine focused on old people; *Life* limps along as an uninfluential monthly. Appealing to a mass audience works only when people cannot gratify their special interests.

Most specialized publications are nowhere near as vulner-

Those who thought they could never go broke underestimating the intelligence of the American people are going to discover that they were wrong.

able as broadcasters. The print media have always been able to target diffuse audiences through subscriptions. They have learned how to compete in a world of custom readership. Magazines are increasingly narrow in their focus, adapted to the special interests of each subscriber.

Spoiled by what was long a captive audience, however, the television networks are sitting ducks for the telecomputer. They will rapidly discover that many of their most successful shows quickly fail when faced with any serious alternatives. Two-million-dollar-a-year anchor people will find that there are hundreds of ways for people to get the news without listening to them.

A new age of individualism is coming, and it will bring an eruption of culture unprecedented in human history. Every film will be able to reach cheaply a potential audience of hundreds of millions of people around the world. For major movie releases, we may even be able to return to the era of the 25-cent premiere. For films appealing to elites, the price will be higher but below that of current movie tickets. Lower prices will expand the ranks of creators and the audiences. The upsurge in artistic output will enhance the position of the United States as the center of video production and creation. We will discover that television was a technology with supreme powers but deadly flaws. In the beginning the powers were ascendant; now the flaws dominate. The cultural limitations of television, tolerable when there was no alternative, are unendurable in the face of the new computer technologies now on the horizon—technologies in which, happily, the U.S. leads the world.

The television industry is not going to give up without a fight. In America, the broadcasters are marshaling their forces to preserve what they claim are the special virtues of free and universal broadcast service. The cable industry is working to prevent the phone companies from installing fiber-optic networks. Television manufacturers around the world are holding out the promise of what they call high-definition television, which is the old spud-farm medium dressed up with a bigger screen and sharper pictures.

Like the rulers of radio in 1950, all the entrenched interests are declaring that the new technology of the telecomputer is unlikely to have an impact for a decade or two. Even computer firms hesitate to compete for this vast potential in the home market. These American companies best able to bring about the age of the telecomputer are cowed by the political forces arrayed against them. By delaying a strong commitment to the new technology, business leaders are simply abdicating technological leadership to the Japanese.

Like all major industrial advances, the telecomputer is an instrument of creative destruction. All the likely victims are mobilizing to prevent their own destruction. It is unsure how soon the creators will win. But their first victories will probably be achieved over technologies less formidable than the TV. Perhaps the first industry to fall before the domonetic tide will be the centralized on-line database.

1:30 PM, Milano, Italy. Courier making deliveries.

The Federal Express worldwide network provides on-time delivery of your express packages in over 120 countries on six continents.

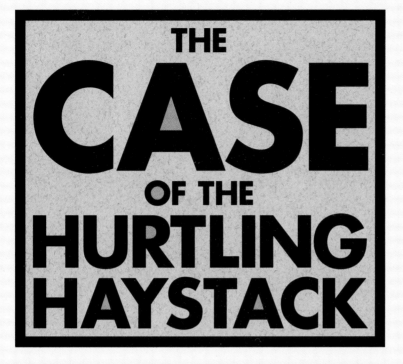

THE CASE OF THE HURTLING HAYSTACK

Standing behind all the new laws of the network that are transforming the telecommunications, computer, and television industries is one simple rule of micro-electronics: Switches and connections on a chip are abundant and cheap, but wires leading from the chip to the outside world are scarce and costly. A single chip, containing hundreds of thousands or even millions of switches and wires, will command at most only a few hundred off-chip connections, and usually only 16 to 48. A fabulous engine of digital processing, the microchip must keep mostly to itself.

The number of connections on a chip is almost doubling every year, but the number of wires leading off the chip is rising at a painfully slow pace. This means that the processing power of individual chips is growing much faster than their communications power. The result is to place a high and fast-rising premium on distributed computing—putting the switches, the intelligence, and the processing power on the customer's desk.

Fiber optics can accelerate this trend. By increasing bandwidth and extending the distance that signals can travel, fiber fuels the movement of switching power to the periphery. Information in the system will move more and more under its own power and at its own rhythm.

Paradoxically, fiber may reduce the power of telecommunications-network owners. Just as the U.S. highway system enhanced the freedom and options of automobile owners, the national fiber-highway system will enhance the freedom and power of communicators. The move from copper wires to fiber-optic threads, however, represents an expansion of power millions of times greater than the move from small streets to gigantic thoroughfares. The power moves increasingly to the drivers on the network rather than to its builders and managers. Any network controlled by a central switching-and-computing system becomes less tenable every year.

This overwhelming trend means that the world of electronics is full of zombie systems. Most people imagine that these electronic systems are young and thriving—even futuristic—when in fact they are in the process of protracted decline. Along with broadcast television, the pyramids of cable TV, mainframe computing, mass manufacturing, and the centralized telephone system are facing decline or even extinction.

In most immediate peril are the centralized on-line database services that dominate the world of information-sharing. These services, from Mead Corporation's Nexis to Knight-Ridder's Dialog, provide access to an immense trove of information—from business data to newspaper archives—stored in large computer-disk memories and reached through telephone lines. Dialog, for example, provides access to 130 million records in 320 huge data libraries or data banks. These records include Dun & Bradstreet financial reports on millions of businesses, abstracts of scientific papers, lists of all government calls for bids on construction contracts, long skeins of regulations in the Federal Register, back issues of hundreds of magazines and other publications, and many other items. This information would indeed be valuable if it could be made efficiently available to the customer.

Database services are said to be on-line because they can be tapped at any time through individual computers. This is called a gateway system. Too many companies, however, imagine that a big computer with a large-capacity memory and a lot of wires constitutes a major information gateway. It is actually more like an information bottleneck.

This world of information-sharing will be overturned. Participating in the revolution is Peter Sprague, chairman of National Semiconductor and CEO of Cryptologics International Inc. To bring about a major change in any mode of service, society always needs entrepreneurs like Sprague.

Like most paths to immense opportunity, the road to Cryptologics began with a problem. In this case, it was the humbling problem of finding a needle in a haystack. More precisely, it was the problem of finding a handful of needles in thousands of haystacks hurtling through the air at nearly the speed of light.

No sweat, thought Peter Sprague two years ago. *Do it with microchips*. This insight came to him in the spring of 1988, shortly after he had moved into National Semiconductor's midtown Manhattan office. At the time, National was struggling in its prime business of microchip production, an enterprise of some $2 billion in annual sales that Sprague had helped launch as a young man of 26. That creative high point had occurred nearly a quarter-century ago. Since then, even as National's revenues had risen, its stock had dropped, as had that of many other high-technology firms. Some of National's investors were beginning to ask what Sprague had done for them lately.

The temporary answer was to become a salesman for National's billion-dollar subsidiary, National Advanced Systems, which sold Hitachi mainframes and software. By selling more Japanese computers, the company could gain time and profits to get its chip operations in order. Selling Japanese computers was not exactly what Sprague had in mind for the rest of his life, but the job led him to a radical idea that could eventually transform the business of distributing data.

In preparation for his new sales responsibilities, Sprague set to work learning about Hitachi's top customers in New York. There were 27 potential Hitachi mainframe purchasers, including owners who might want to upgrade their systems. Sprague asked the California sales office to get information on these customers' financial condition from Knight-Ridder's Dialog Service. In the end, he decided instead to get information on the business of Dialog.

The basic principle of on-line systems like Dialog is toll-taking. The owners of these systems set up mainframe computers and connect them to immense databases. Whenever a customer logs on to the system through the telephone, looking for information, the meter starts ticking. These companies whop customers with large charges for logging on, searching, getting lost, using national networks and phone lines, for consultation, as well as for the information they receive—if they are lucky enough to get any.

When Peter Sprague asked for information from Dialog, an employee in National's California office got him the specified dope on the financial condition of eight companies. Then she learned that getting an inch-high pile of often redundant or out-of-date materials on eight firms had already run up a bill of more than $3,000. To continue the search on 19 other companies might eventually cost more than $10,000.

In the mazes of Dialog, Sprague had stumbled onto what might be called a gateway data trap. For some routine data on 27 firms, Dialog was ready to charge about the same amount it would cost him to buy a computer with a hard-disk memory, together with a compact disc read-only memory (CD-ROM) system and a scanner that could process acres of print—all of which would fit conveniently on his desk. The hard-disk memory could hold dozens of megabytes of information, or the amount of data contained in more than one hundred books; the CD-ROM could hold gigabytes of information, or the amount of data contained in thousands of books. The information Sprague was looking for was not yet available on CD-ROM, but he felt it would be as soon as the market expanded.

The entire world of on-line databases was an absurd anachronism.

In domonetic terms, the problem Sprague encountered with Dialog was simple. Dialog is a centralized network run by a mainframe. It puts the brains at the top of the hierarchy and treats the customer like a dumb terminal. Everywhere in the new domonetic world, the brains were moving to the bottom, or to the fringes, of the hierarchy—to the customer premises, to the user's desktop, to the viewer's VCR. Dialog was defying the centrifugal force of microelectronics sweeping through all of information technology.

Dialog was not an exception; the entire world of on-line databases was an absurd anachronism. The systems could conduct only one search at a time. Customers had to pay for their minutes on-line, even if they didn't find anything they wanted. Because of the time required to integrate new data, the information that customers finally got was often out of date.

Only about one-tenth of the charges usually pertained to the actual information customers received; all the rest was for phone use and searches. Moreover, customers had to subscribe to the entire system with its 320 databases, even if they wanted only an occasional "hit" of information. At a time when putting computing power and storage on every desk was cheap, this system concentrated the intelligence in one place and ran wires to and from it. At a time when having thousands of computers searching in parallel around the world was cheap, this system had customers queuing up around the world to use a single computer. Sprague had run into a network anomaly: a top-down structure in a bottom-up world.

In a deeper sense, however, the chairman of National had come face-to-face with the central problem of the information age. Computers multiply data; in fact, one study indicates that data will double 19 times before the year 2000. How will anyone be able to find the information he needs in this huge haystack? The world is already choking on data.

T. S. Eliot addressed the problem in his poem "The Rock":

> Where is the Life we have lost in living?
> Where is the wisdom we have lost in knowledge?
> Where is the knowledge we have lost in information?

One might add: Where is the information we have lost in data?

No one denies that the immense gains in the power of computers have yet to yield similar advances in the power of people to find and use information. The use of on-line databases such as Dialog in particular has fallen far short of expectations.

These systems are still used by relatively few people at relatively high prices, and much of the data have inestimable worth. Indeed, most of the time, no one—including the database companies that try to sell access to it—bothers to calculate their worth. Database expert Alfred Glossbrenner, author of *How to Look it up Online*, declares, "You don't have to spend much time perusing the rate cards of the various vendors to realize that the information industry hasn't the slightest idea how to price its products."

The failure of these systems is not hard to comprehend. On-line databases require the customer to use a telephone line hooked to a computer terminal to request specific information from a mainframe. Each database requires special protocols and commands, in some cases adding up to more than 10 steps, which take substantial effort to master. The Dialog manual, for instance, contains more than 700 pages of detailed instructions on how to use the system. Only information specialists can use these systems efficiently, and each specialist is normally an expert on only one system.

After logging on and specifying the needed information, the user must stay on-line while the mainframe searches through a number of memory banks, which are often scattered among smaller databases also connected by telephone lines. Telephone charges alone often compose from one-third to one-half the operating costs of an on-line database company.

As a result, the proliferation of information technology has created data overload. In Eliot's terms, the vast stores of data rarely reach the level of usable information. The information of the information age remains trapped in hierarchical pyramids, accessed laboriously by large computers and transmitted only slowly and inefficiently to the people who need it.

Through his experience with Dialog, Peter Sprague had encountered the problem of information that was available but unavailing. Pondering this problem, he found a way to break open the information bottleneck and flatten the data pyramids. Sprague recalled an experience with QuoTrek, a product he had tried to rescue when he was a venture capitalist. QuoTrek, produced by the Dataspeed Corporation, had offered specific stock-market quotes, chosen by the user

1:12 AM, Memphis, Tennessee. Packages clearing customs.

Sending a package to or from a foreign land?
Federal Express knows the customs, so your package is delivered on time —
without unnecessary delays.

2:11 PM, Indianapolis, Indiana. Loading Heavyweight[SM] shipments.

We handle virtually any size package
to virtually any destination. In fact, the Federal Express system handles
up to 14 million pounds daily.

through a hand-held terminal that tapped sideband FM radio frequencies. Because these sidebands border the frequencies used by FM stations, they have to be kept free of audio signals to prevent interference between stations. In the early 1980s, however, the Federal Communications Commission approved the sending of data over these fallow portions of FM bandwidth.

The little QuoTrek machine, simple as it was, differed drastically from all other on-line systems. It required no intelligence at the information source; stock-market quotes were broadcast indiscriminately on the sideband network. The intelligence was contained in the hand-held QuoTrek tuner. This small black box, resembling a radio with an antenna, was tuned to the radio frequencies through which QuoTrek transmitted its information. Customers keyed in the name of a stock on which they wanted price updates, and the tuner filtered out all the other information flowing through the frequency. The prices appeared on a small screen on the hand-held terminal.

The hand-held Quo-Trek tuner was the first device that customers could use to scan broadcast data themselves.

This tuner was practically a toy compared with today's scanners. Sprague knew that more advanced microprocessors (computers on microchips) could scan much greater streams of more varied information—whole hurtling haystacks of data. A company could broadcast information in large quantities and let customers scan it on the fly at their desks. Together, the two sidebands of one FM station could transmit 100 million words of data a day, or about the content of 1,000 full-length books. This would be like transmitting almost one book every minute and a half all day long and searching them for key words: a rate that is well within the capacity of current microelectronic scanners.

With the modest notion of using the available sidebands of one FM station and the scanning capacity of one microchip, Sprague had found a way of giving the customer daily access to specific data from whole encyclopedias of information. All it would take was an implementation of the mandate of the microcosm: move intelligence from large centralized systems into the hands of customers.

Sprague was too excited to keep the idea to himself. He

called a meeting with William Walker, a lawyer and former U.S. Deputy Trade Representative. Walker said that if Sprague was interested in database access, he should meet another client who was stopping by the office. Walker introduced Sprague to Thomas Lipscomb, the former head of the New York Times Book Company and of Downe Communications, who impressed Sprague by instantly recognizing the value of his idea.

During several intense discussions between Sprague and Lipscomb, the idea grew into a business plan for a new corporation, called Cryptologics International Inc., which would be devoted to launching a radically new mode of data distribution. The company would produce a scanner resembling the QuoTrek device, but it would use the far more

Information-system entrepreneurs Thomas Lipscomb (left) and Peter Sprague are trying to tumble the pyramids of the on-line database industry with the launch of Cryptologics International Inc.

powerful technology then available. The company would broadcast a flow of data and sell the scanners, which could be plugged into desktop computers. As in the QuoTrek system, customers could key in a description of the data they wanted, but with Cryptologics they could specify much more. They could use up to 2,000 words to describe exactly what they wanted.

Cryptologics would broadcast the data in encrypted form, and customers could decrypt the data they had specified simply by pressing a key on the scanner. The new system would charge customers only for the decrypted and retrieved information, rather than for the entire service as systems like Dialog do now. A record of the information decrypted by customers would automatically be entered into the memories of their computers, which Cryptologics could tap to calculate charges.

Sprague and Lipscomb's concept could bring the microcosmic revolution fully to the database arena. By allowing the customer to pay only for the information used rather than for the time on-line and for the entire database, Cryptologics could release immense volumes of data currently trapped on disks, tapes, microfilm, and cassettes, and in libraries around the globe.

Cryptologics could, for example, regularly distribute to lawyers the Federal Register or the Tax Code encrypted on CD-ROMs and then broadcast updates to them. The company's software can quickly integrate new information with data previously stored on the customers' CD-ROMs. The customers would pay only for each use of the disks or broadcasts. Cryptologics could also distribute archives of encyclopedias, technical standards, magazines, and newspapers on disks, update them by broadcast, and charge only when the user accessed a specific item.

This technology could drastically increase the income of the creators of information. Today the bulk of the money from information-sharing goes to the distributors—to the owners of the database and the mainframe computers that access it, and the phone companies that provide the lines. With Cryptologics' incomparably cheaper desktop device, which identifies exactly what is being used and stores a record in memory, specific royalties could flow to the writer and publisher of each article each time it was decrypted. At present, most information-providers have no way of determining which articles by which authors are accessed.

The producers of information, from newspapers to financial-data publishing firms, could also gain huge new benefits. The expense and inefficiency of current modes of data distribution greatly restrict their potential markets. A system like Cryptologics could link publishers with their customers far more efficiently, thus expanding opportunities for both. Information-producers could cheaply provide the exact material sought by customers, who could then spend their time reading it rather than wasting their time scanning material in hopes of finding what they needed. The Cryptologics box, rather than the customer, would do the scanning.

As Eliot also observed, however, between the idea and the act falls the shadow. Sprague and Lipscomb needed technical experts and financial partners to execute their plans. They also needed to prepare for the threat that they would pose to all the centralized systems of data distribution.

Hanging above Peter Sprague's desk is a quotation from Machiavelli's *The Prince*, which explains the obstacles to innovation: "It must be remembered that there is nothing more difficult to plan, more doubtful of success, nor more dangerous to manage than the creation of a new system. For the initiator has the enmity of all who would profit by the preservation of the old institutions and merely lukewarm defenders in those who would gain by the new ones."

Machiavelli's theories of innovation, presented in *The Prince* in 1513, still apply to today's information society.

Information technology has advanced many millionfold since Machiavelli wrote this in 1513, but no writer has better summed up the predicament of innovators. Even though capitalism gives a voice and a present value to the interests of the future, defending the past remains easier for most people. Capitalism may offer the promise of great power and wealth to the very few people who can shape or anticipate the future, but bureaucratic politics provides a rich panoply of weapons to the many more people who want to resist change. Whenever possible, the government and its principalities attempt to frustrate or dispossess innovators.

The Machiavellian truth, therefore, remains a central problem for Peter Sprague and most other American innovators. It leads to a complementary truth voiced by Peter F. Drucker, Machiavelli's visionary 20th-century counterpart. On grounds similar to Machiavelli's, Drucker contends that no new system can displace an established system unless it outperforms it by a factor of 10. Otherwise, the established system will have enough money, momentum, expertise, legal clout, capital plant, installed base, and satisfied customers to hold off the new concept.

Sprague and Lipscomb are still in the process of launching a radical new system for distributing all forms of data. For its chosen purposes, the system outperforms its established rivals by a factor of hundreds or even thousands. Thus, the system should be both supremely disruptive and hugely redemptive. It is the kind of innovation that Joseph Schumpeter had in mind when he coined the term *creative destruction*.

To execute the plan, Cryptologics has attracted some of the most formidable talent in electronics. John R. Michener, a quantum physicist, materials scientist, and engineer who formerly held prominent research-and-development positions at Kodak and Siemens, is designing the hardware, encryption devices, and decryption chips. The project planner is James Parker, a former CBS executive who had been in charge of the network's role in the Prodigy system. This system, which is now being launched by IBM and Sears after CBS's withdrawal from the project, allows owners of personal computers to shop for retail goods in a large, computerized database. If it can overcome the slowness of its system, Prodigy can create a national electronics market in which distribution costs can be drastically cut and prices greatly reduced.

Like the interactive networks of personal-computer workstations, Sprague's technology moves with the new domonetic tide. Springing from the new microelectronic technologies of computation and storage, it radically changes the locus of data control and profit. It shifts power from the distributors of data to its users and creators.

As American innovators, Sprague and Lipscomb face some of the world's most hostile capital markets. High capital-gains taxes and a loss–deductibility limit of $3,000 a year constitute almost prohibitive penalties on risk-taking by individual investors. This bizarre combination of punishing both success and failure has resulted in American investors' fleeing high-technology investments. Initial public offerings have nearly halted for risky businesses, in general, and small computer-related firms have price-earnings ratios well below the Dow Jones industrials.

Under these circumstances, venture capitalists and other

New desktop computing systems will allow the world to capture the information lost in today's immense trove of data.

investors tend to focus on leveraged buyouts and the financing of established companies. Entrepreneurs like Sprague and Lipscomb are forced to pursue foreign money and big corporate investors. Raising funds from these sources is a delicate matter, for Sprague and Lipscomb have to persuade them to invest without buying their company outright. "In search of princes, I have kissed so many frogs," Sprague complains, "I am all but dripping with frog goo."

Sprague and Lipscomb are launching Cryptologics with a total of $750,000 from 10 individual venturers, and they are in the process of raising some $15 million more. Sprague hopes that the system can eventually be financed by information-producers looking for ways to expand their markets.

Cryptologics is still being launched; it is not yet a service. Its promise is great, but the execution may still be fumbled. Regardless of the outcome, Cryptologics provides a powerful example of the kinds of new technologies that are emerging to challenge the centralized stronghold of current information systems.

Intelligent scanner technology not only threatens mainframe gateways and data traps but also highlights the vulnerability of some phone companies' grand plans to become the chief channel for new computer-data and business-information services. By using the rich resources of specialized computing power both in the network and on the customer's desk, Cryptologics manages, for some purposes, to simulate and even improve upon the digitally switched networks of the phone company. Transmitting the contents of a CD-ROM through the fastest current fax machine, for example, would take a phone company six full days.

The telephone companies cannot prevail with their centralized systems. They must complement the massive movement of intelligence to customers' desktops by vastly expanding the bandwidths of their systems with fiber optics. A new fiber network would foster a more rapid distribution of intelligence throughout the world by greatly increasing the communications power of small computers. This development is the true destiny of telecommunications, and it must be the telephone companies' urgent goal in the information age.

10:05 AM, Portland, Oregon. The Powership 2 system speaks directly to our
Memphis computer, eliminating the need for airbills and manifests.

Used by over 7,000 companies to streamline
the shipping process, the Powership 2® system places the power of
the Federal Express computer at your fingertips.

LET THERE BE LIGHT

Aluminum wires! Richard Snelling, then an engineering director at Southern Bell, could hardly believe his ears. He had come all the way from Atlanta to New Jersey, to the very top of the AT&T Bell pyramid, only to hear from an AT&T scientist that the telephone industry would soon have to replace copper telephone wires with aluminum.

The year was 1975, and the world was running out of natural resources, said the AT&T pundit. Everyone knew that oil was scarce, but that was only the beginning of the dire scenario of depletion and scarcity that he was describing. Soon the world would be stripped of copper.

Even AT&T's famous Carbon Mountain was shriveling to a pathetic black pile. Carbon Mountain contained the world's last available reserves of carbon pure enough to be used in the devices that convert voice pressures to electrical signals in telephone mouthpieces. After the depletion of carbon, the AT&T man said, copper would be next.

He said that aluminum wire was the only realistic alternative to copper. Aluminum, a good conductor of electricity, is also one of the earth's most abundant metals. The only other remotely possible alternative, he added, was fiber-optic cables, but engineers were decades away from producing silica glass pure enough to serve the telephone network.

Snelling did not like the idea of using aluminum wire, especially in the South. He knew that aluminum would corrode faster than copper, because it was more chemically active. Even copper didn't last long in a region with high temperatures, high humidity, high water tables, and frequent electrical storms. Snelling was not about to authorize the adoption of aluminum for his system.

As a phone-company engineer in the booming new South, Snelling was unaccustomed to shrinking horizons. During his rise through the ranks of Southern Bell, he had viewed the company's ever-widening vistas as the essence of telephony. Snelling, who had served for several years as a spokesman for AT&T, giving speeches at colleges, high schools, and Rotary Clubs around the South, had hailed a veritable new age in electronics, rich with new technology springing from inventions at AT&T's Bell Laboratories.

The transistor and the laser had both come from Bell Labs,

Richard Snelling, an executive vice-president at Southern Bell, is a global crusader in the drive to run fiber-optic cables to the home.

and the company's researchers had recently made key contributions to the development of fiber optics. MIT professor Claude Shannon, a communications theorist who had spent most of his career at Bell Labs, had provided the conceptual foundations for all digital networks. His system showed how to transmit voice and video signals and computer data in digital form, store the information when needed, and switch it through the network's interconnections. This high-capacity, or "broadband," system, now called an integrated services digital network (ISDN), is perfectly suited for fiber optics.

Shannon's research had shown that over time an entirely digital network would cost about half as much to run and maintain as the traditional Bell system, which converted voice pressures to analog waves. Snelling had been told, however, that under the financial pressures of mid-1970s recession, AT&T was cutting back on investments in such new technologies as fiber optics and digital switching. This deeply distressed Snelling, since he had gotten into the telephone business in the first place because of its technological promise.

Claude Shannon's theories of communication provided the conceptual foundations for all digital networks.

The son of a milliner, Snelling had watched the market for women's hats collapse despite his mother's heroic efforts. "It was the kind of business that no matter what you did," Snelling said, "you knew sales would be lower next year than this year." Going from copper to aluminum reminded him of women's hats. Since fiber optics was the only alternative, Snelling decided to look into that. He began an intense study of the science, practice, and promise of the new technology. He soon learned that the AT&T scientist had been wrong in his prediction that decades would pass before fiber could be used in the telephone system. Far from being a remote prospect, the technology was already available from Corning Glass. Snelling became a global crusader in the move to fiber optics in telephony.

He would have a hard time, though, getting his colleagues at AT&T excited about fiber. The phone company during the 1970s and 1980s was not an entrepreneurial force. Headed by a clique of Midwestern good old boys led by CEO John deButts and later by CEO Charles Brown, the telephone company specialized mainly in public service and public relations.

In truth, the nation's politicians wanted it that way. As a public utility, AT&T dispensed a reliable flow of dividends to senior citizens, created affirmative-action jobs for favored constituents, contributed to charities and political-campaign coffers, and spent billions of dollars on law firms, lobbyists, economists, and social-policy consultants. The phone company had become bovine: the great all-American cash cow to be milked and massaged, prodded and sued, and milked again.

AT&T was not even allowed to invest aggressively. It was a monopoly regulated by the Federal Communications Commission and 50 state public-utilities commissions, hounded relentlessly by the Antitrust Division of the Justice Department, and watched over by the gimlet eyes of Congress and federal, state, and municipal judges. In an ultimately self-defeating effort to keep down the price of phone service, the FCC and state authorities required AT&T to assume, for accounting-depreciation purposes, that the useful life of phone-company equipment was as long as 40 to 50 years. Thus, AT&T was obligated to treat its installed base of plant and equipment more as a historical object to be preserved than as a competitive weapon in the global struggle for the future of teletechnology.

During this time, the structure of the U.S. telephone system resembled a pyramid. Peter Huber, a leading telecommunications consultant and author of *The Geodesic Network*, described it well: "Customer-premises equipment was primitive and occupied a correspondingly humble position at the very lowest level. . . . Arrayed above in a rigid hierarchy lay the five tiers of the AT&T switching system [numbered simply from five at the bottom to one at the top]. Thousands of class-five switches served as local-end offices. A handful of class-one switches were located at the apex, providing the highest levels of national coordination and control. Three intermediate tiers of switching lay in between. The structure had the solidity, permanence, and inflexibility of the Great Pyramid, which on paper it resembled."

Putting the customer at the bottom did not mean he got a bad deal. As a matter of fact, this was a way of putting the

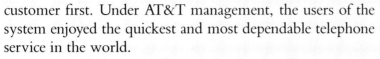

customer first. Under AT&T management, the users of the system enjoyed the quickest and most dependable telephone service in the world.

A pyramid is the optimal network when intelligence is concentrated at the top. In the Bell system, intelligence was clearly concentrated in New Jersey, at the headquarters of AT&T, at the manufacturing facilities of Western Electric, and at Bell Laboratories, the world's greatest research institution.

New Jersey was the top of the pyramid. The Bell elite designed and manufactured new equipment, developed new technology for military and space applications, laid plans for long-distance and international service, conceived regulatory strategies, and trafficked with diplomats and politicians. This was the exalted domain of telecommunications. At the bottom were the regional offices that provided what the telephone people called POTS, or plain old telephone service.

The regional divisions of AT&T, like Southern Bell, and their local subsidiaries did the grunt work—installing phones, digging holes, pulling wire through underground conduits, climbing poles, and dealing with the effects of electrical storms. Snelling was proud to be a POTS man, but most people at AT&T regarded phone service as somehow demeaning. It was a distraction amid all the shining opportunities and technologies of the information society, from office automation and satellites to aerospace communications and microelectronics, which were then being cultivated at Bell Labs.

From the top of the pyramid, change at the POTS level was viewed as a threat. Although the research-and-development arm of AT&T was radically progressive, the attitude of the company's managers was what anyone might expect from a group working under the government's equipment-depreciation schedules. Except for the carefully measured, step-by-step replacement of old equipment with more advanced gear from Western Electric, any new devices attached to the network seemed only to menace the intricate and seamless system of customer service.

For its time, this conservatism was appropriate. The pyramidal structure of the phone company—like the similar pyramids of broadcast-television and mainframe-computer networks—was the best that could have been engineered. As in computer networks, the telephone system operates through a vast mesh of wires and switches. Wires largely determine the bandwidth of the system, or its communications power. Switches chiefly provide the system's intelligence.

Network architectures may be composed of many wires and a few switches or many switches and a few wires. In terms of the telephone system, these two extremes mean attaching millions of phones to one continuous ring of wire with a switch at each phone, or attaching millions of phones through millions of wires to a central switching system. AT&T had chosen the more centralized system, with wires running from every household to the switches of the central office. One regional-office switching system could serve about 15,000 phones.

Until the upsurge of microelectronics during the 1970s and 1980s, this system made sense. Wires were cheap and reliable, and their bandwidth was sufficient for voice communication, which was the overwhelming bulk of the business. Switches, on the other hand, were then expensive electromechanical and electronic devices.

A few superbly crafted switches at the top of the pyramid shifted calls through millions of wires. The Bell pyramid channeled thousands of wires into central offices, where the calls were switched, first by the familiar operator plugging patch cords into switchboards, later by magnetically controlled switches, and finally by expensive computers. The pyramid was not only the best option; it was really the only option.

To most AT&T executives, the only real threat to this supremely reliable and efficient system seemed to be an antitrust suit from the U.S. Department of Justice, which claimed that the company was an illegal monopoly. Snelling, however, had already sensed that the Bell pyramid was doomed. Its nemesis was not the Antitrust Division of the Justice Department but the research-and-development division of AT&T itself. Through the creation of powerful microelectronic devices and processes, beginning with the tran-

11:35 PM, Memphis, Tennessee. Charter flights assigned.

If your domestic or overseas freight shipments require
customized service, Federal Express offers air charter service with our
fleet of B-747s, DC-10s and B-727s.

sistor in 1948, Bell Labs had drastically decreased the cost of switches in relation to wires, thus subverting the economic foundations of the pyramid.

When Snelling joined the company in 1956, a simple transistor switch cost about $7. By the mid-1970s, the time of the copper crisis, a much faster and better transistor cost about three one-hundredths of a cent. A decade later, a transistor cost a little more than one ten-thousandth of a cent.

Switches had practically become a free good, while, in relative terms, the price of copper wires had skyrocketed. While almost no one was looking, Bell Labs had completely overturned the balance of expense and efficiency in wires and switches—the pivot on which the architecture of the entire network was based.

The ideal network suddenly turned out to be a minimum number of wires with the switches—and thus the intelligence—situated in the nation's private homes and offices, which were linked to the regional phone offices. Switching systems would someday be incorporated into every phone, television, computer, fax machine, and database, all of which, in essence, might be connected to one continuous ring of wire. This notion is less farfetched than it may seem. A system such as this would resemble those used for local-area computer networks. AT&T, MCI, U.S. Sprint, and other long-distance companies would eventually have to compete with the Baby Bells, independent phone companies, and computer firms for part of the ring.

Richard Snelling knew that this ring structure could eventually transform his business. If he had anything to do with it, Southern Bell would operate through a ring of fiber-optic cable, not through copper or aluminum wire. With his combination of long experience in the field and a deep grounding in Claude Shannon's communications theory, which he taught in AT&T classes, Snelling would provide crucial impetus to the coming revolution in technology and culture.

By 1978, soon after fiber became available for use in the telephone system, Snelling began using these glass wires to replace the decaying parts of his copper network. Since Southern Bell was a regulated business, he had to demonstrate to the FCC and the Public Utilities Commission that fiber was economically sound and would not push up telephone rates. Snelling presented data that proved the economic viability of fiber. He showed that the incredible reliability and capacity of the glass, with its low maintenance costs and immunity to corrosion and lightning, justified the investment in Southern communities. By 1979, Snelling had installed fiber-optic cables throughout most of northwestern Atlanta, running them to a point within 2,600 feet of the customers' homes.

While almost no one was looking, Bell Labs had completely overturned the balance of expense and efficiency in wires and switches.

In the larger AT&T scheme, however, Snelling's venture in glass represented a modest experiment. He could not persuade his bosses in New Jersey to make a more general commitment to the new technology. In the early 1980s, AT&T was not using fiber in most of its long-distance lines. Japan was committed to a long-distance network made entirely of fiber and had launched a number of experiments with fiber to the home. France was undergoing a drive to entirely digitize its system. Sweden's highly digitized national network was the most efficient in the world, charging less than half what the U.S. billed customers for local calls. AT&T's Bell Labs was the world's leading innovator in telephony, but the company was falling further and further behind the rest of the world in the application of new technology. Deterring the firm from any aggressive move were thousands of lawyers, judges, commissioners, and politicians fostering an entrenched culture of timidity and slow write-offs.

With AT&T slow in installing the new technology, the U.S. was on the verge of losing leadership not only in switching equipment but also in the manufacture of fiber. Corning Glass had spent nearly 17 years perfecting the processes for manufacturing the ultra-pure fibers that were necessary for long-distance service. But the industry had hit an impasse. Two kinds of interference in the glass—known as chromatic and modal dispersion—greatly reduced the distance that signals could be sent without expensive repeaters. Then, at a time when a solution to this problem seemed remote, Corning scientists made a technological breakthrough. They discovered that by using a different type of fiber, called single-mode fiber, the modal dispersion was eliminated. In addition, they found that the chromatic dispersion was reduced to zero at a specific infrared wavelength easily created by existing lasers. These discoveries vastly increased the amount of information that could be carried and extended the distance the signals could be transmitted. The breakthrough was comparable only to the discovery that silicon could be both electrically insulated and chemically protected by its own oxide—a finding that was crucial to the development of microelectronics.

During the early 1980s, however, few managers in the upper ranks of AT&T were interested in using this radical new technology to replace the copper and microwave systems used for long-distance calls. Their reluctance made sense, because AT&T was by far the leader in the global installed base of copper and microwave systems. The network dwarfed Japan's and was nearly as large as all the other phone networks in the world put together. If fiber were to replace copper and microwave systems, AT&T would suffer by far the most.

The company had become a crenelated fortress with little awareness that its most cherished strategies and assumptions were radically outdated. A global campaign was already under way to seize leadership from the U.S. in electronic technology. Few Americans comprehended that telecommunications was becoming the coveted prize in this global struggle. The nations that most rapidly expanded their networks of fiber-optic wires and switches, reaching out to labyrinthine mazes of digital computers and other electronic equipment, would dominate the new age of information sweeping the global economy.

Of the people who did understand these new domonetic realities, the Japanese were the most vigorous in reaching toward them. They had been avidly following the fiber-optic breakthroughs at Corning and AT&T and were reproducing them in Japan. As early as 1982, Fujitsu Limited began manufacturing fiber systems that outperformed AT&T's. Only the intervention of the U.S. government, acting on grounds of national security, prevented Fujitsu from beating out AT&T's Western Electric in a bid to build the vital fiber-optic systems between Boston, New York, and Washington, D.C.

The Japanese government had launched no fewer than three major research projects in the field of digital telecommunications, sustaining an effort even greater than its celebrated projects in semiconductor technology. NTT, Japan's phone company, was planning a new national fiber network, encompassing entire cities with Japanese-made fiber and digital switching equipment. It had targeted the year 2000 for completion of the system. To reach that goal, NEC, which supplies most of NTT's equipment, is using Japanese scientists trained at Bell Labs to make it a world leader in optoelectronics, the technology for coupling electronic computers to photonic fiber systems.

Although Japan commanded a network only one-third as

William McGowan, president of MCI, came to the rescue of American telecommunications when he purchased enough fiber from Corning Glass to help make it a global leader in fiber-optic technology.

large as America's and produced only one-third the telecommunications equipment, it seemed poised to take the global lead in the industry. Corning seemed likely to join RCA and Ampex in the growing catalog of American firms that were losing their supreme inventions to Japan. Sumitomo Electric Industries was directly copying the Corning process, and NTT was adopting the technology. American courts—so fierce in suppressing the illusory aggressions of AT&T— stood inert before the wholesale looting of technology by Japanese manufacturers and refused to stop the importation of fiber optics. The American position in this central technology of the information age was rapidly eroding and, except for a few lonely pioneers like Richard Snelling, no one was stepping forth to halt the slide.

In his 1982 Modified Final Judgment, Judge Harold Greene broke apart the phone-company monopoly.

Salvation came from an unlikely source: the U.S. government. Acting through the antitrust arm of the Justice Department, Washington forced the breakup of the telephone company. Announced in 1982 and phased in over the following two years, this judicial action, presided over by Judge Harold Greene, was enormously complex. In essence, it assigned to AT&T the role of long-distance service and telecommunications-equipment manufacturing. It also created seven regional operating companies—Pacific Telesis, U.S. West, Southwestern Bell Corporation, Bell-South, Ameritech, Bell Atlantic, and Nynex—known as the Baby Bells, to do the grunt work of POTS.

In some ways, deregulation was not logical. Local telephone service is a textbook case of a natural monopoly. Particularly in fiber-optic networks, incremental costs are virtually zero; no money needs to be spent to install new lines to the home or maintain the existing plant. Once the system is built, there are hardly any long-term limits to the amount of traffic it can hold. Therefore, the company with the greatest market share, and thus the lowest costs, will be able to drive out all of its competitors. Yet the U.S. was holding a free-for-all race to enter the field of long-distance service.

Logical or not, the breakup called forth two improbable saviors for American telecommunications competitiveness.

2:33 PM, Singapore. Afternoon deliveries on their way.

Federal Express delivers over 1.5 million packages
throughout the world. Every day.

One was William McGowan, president of MCI. This company, which had $230 million in revenues in 1981, had based its entire long-distance telephone network on microwave technology. The second savior was Michael Milken, Drexel Burnham Lambert's junk-bond king, who had virtually no experience in the telecommunications business.

McGowan recognized the possibilities of long-distance fiber-optic telecommunications, and he was determined to utilize the new technology. The only problem was that the national network he had in mind would cost as much as $3 billion. Michael Milken saved the day by offering to finance the project with the vast resources of his new market in high-yield securities known as junk bonds. Milken even persuaded McGowan to increase his public offering from $500 million to $1 billion. At the time, this was the largest public offering in history. Over the next several years, Milken raised nearly $2 billion more for MCI.

With the Milken financing in hand, McGowan ordered 62,112 miles of the most advanced fiber from Corning. This huge order gave Corning the resources to streamline its production process, placing its technology ahead of Sumitomo and NTT. Corning thus managed to maintain its worldwide lead and market share in the technology it had pioneered and pursued for 17 years.

MCI also spurred AT&T to launch a major fiber drive. Faced with sudden, massive competition, the bound Prometheus of American telecommunications finally got moving. By 1990, nearly all the long-distance and overseas networks of AT&T were composed of digital fiber-optic lines.

AT&T ended the 1980s by gaining market share around the globe. The U.S. had more than 25 percent more telephones in use per capita than Japan and 15 percent more than Europe, commanded more than half the world's telecommunications revenues, and had more than half the world's installed base of fiber-optic cables.

Together with an even larger dominance in computers, these were the greatest American achievements of the decade. The U.S. began and ended the 1980s with nearly a 70 percent global market share in computers, and it is in a strong position to extend its dominance into the next century. It must wake up to the fact, however, that the world of telecommunications is being overturned by technology.

The focus of competition has shifted from long-distance lines to integrated services digital networks (ISDN) reaching into every home and office. The creation of this network, together with the computer systems that are linked to it and the optoelectronics that make it work, is the key to U.S. competitiveness. Nearly every industrial policy in other developed countries is preparing to face this challenge. The Japanese government has projected total investments of nearly $300 billion to bring this ISDN network to fruition. The U.S. government is doggedly blocking any such achievement in America.

In the early 1980s, the Antitrust Division of the Justice Department was a revitalizing force in U.S. telecommunications. The 1982 Modified Final Judgment, however, now serves to paralyze the system. Judge Harold Greene effectively forbade AT&T, the leading force in telecommunications research and development, from taking fiber networks to the home. The seven Baby Bell holding companies represent a huge potential resource of capital and technology for American competitiveness, but they are not allowed to manufacture telecommunications equipment or use it to provide new services that would pay for fiber to the home. The 50 state public-utilities commissions are concerned chiefly with holding down the price of local service by preventing the Bells from launching major investment programs. Moreover, the U.S. Congress has created cable-television monopolies in every city.

Like the antitrust action against AT&T, the cable companies once provided a force of revitalization. They vastly improved American television. Today the cable operators are primarily myopic entities, milking their monopoly profits and heavily financing the campaigns of politicians who uphold the regulatory structure that protects them. The cable operators, unless they join the digital world, will not only prevent the Baby Bells from fulfilling their manifest destiny to deliver fiber to the home but will also likely aid the Japanese effort in high-definition TV. They propose to lay fiber-optic lines that

Cable operators represent a nearly insuperable obstacle to American competitiveness in telecommunications.

will carry HDTV signals to the home, but these lines will not be compatible with ISDN standards. Cable operators represent a nearly insuperable obstacle to American competitiveness in telecommunications. At a critical juncture in industrial history, U.S. telecommunications is constricted by regulatory pythons.

Although the two million American housing units built each year provide an immediate potential market of at least $2 billion annually for fiber and related technology, investors are not interested in this opportunity. In the late 1980s, Wall Street's hostility toward technological entrepreneurship reached near-pathological levels. As a result, major U.S. microchip-equipment and semiconductor-production companies were being sold off to foreign buyers at fire-sale prices.

Leading U.S. economists urged that the dollar, already crippled in purchasing power, be devalued still further to increase American competitiveness in farm goods and other commodities. Yet a cheaper dollar would increase the price of imported components and equipment on which American manufacturers greatly depend. A cheaper dollar would also devalue U.S. companies' assets, making their cost of raising capital in the global markets among the highest in the world. This ability to raise vast sums of capital, though, would be vital to the drive for delivering fiber to the home and office and critical to national competitiveness.

Richard Snelling, now an executive vice-president at Southern Bell, is battling for the advancement of U.S. telecommunications. At the 1987 GlobeCom conference in Tokyo, Snelling issued a bold statement to American industry. If the government did not want the telephone companies to compete with the precious cable monopolies, so be it, he said. He would run fiber to the customers' homes anyway, if only to lower maintenance costs and improve voice transmission over the telephone. Southern Bell would soon buy no more copper wire or conduits. Snelling hopes that one day his fiber will be used for vastly expanded telecommunications functions. He knows that one way or another the age of the telecomputer is approaching.

Some critics charge that phone rates will rise. This might be true in the short run if Snelling tried to rip up all the copper in the South and run lines to every home. But he will phase in the fiber slowly as economics dictate. In the long run, however, the price of wire telephony and all other communications would rise drastically compared with foreign systems if Snelling failed to install fiber. The U.S. telecommunications system would become a crazy quilt of incompatible analog systems. New technologies will bring phone prices down, unless existing regulations prevent the creation of the most efficient and coherent network—a fiber-optic system.

Other critics fear a new antitrust threat from a fiber telecommunications network. This system, however, would not be anything like a telephone-company monopoly. With the intelligence at the bottom of the pyramid, in a maze of personal computers and private network systems, the American telephone companies would have less control than ever before.

In addition, the huge bandwidth of fiber optics means that phone companies would have no incentive to restrict access to the network. Instead, they would have a great incentive to lower prices until the network was filled.

Wires are no longer the source of monopoly power. Long-distance lines have become a free-for-all for any company with an empty tube or strip of land longer than it is wide. Williams Tele-communications Group Inc., which was launched by Williams Pipe Line Company, has laid fiber inside its decommissioned fuel lines, and it now owns the fourth-largest U.S. fiber network.

Even more significant is the emergence of effective cellular-phone systems that do not use wire at all. While television service is moving increasingly from the air to wire, telephone service is shifting increasingly from wire to the air. Far from being a monopoly threat, fiber to the home is now indispensable in preventing the Baby Bells from losing the key growth markets in telecommunications to cable television and wireless-telephone companies. Under FCC rules, each regional cellular market is shared between the local phone companies and other bidders, but the only coherent national cellular system, Cellular One, is dominated by McCaw Cellular Communications Inc.

Funded in part with junk bonds, like MCI, McCaw Cellular Communications is a vast wireless-telephone system with networks scattered all over the country. This system will be digitized in coming years, making its acoustics better than those of ordinary copper-wire telephone networks. As the electronic switching gear and portable handsets drop in price at the usual pace of silicon technology—about 90 percent every seven years—the wireless system will become fully competitive in price with plug-in telephones. The Baby Bells will then have to lay fiber to the home, with all its amenities, merely to keep their existing position in the industry.

When personal pocket phones are more convenient, higher in sound quality, and just as cheap as fixed telephones, they will become the preferred service. Before that happens, the Baby Bells must make a massive entrepreneurial move to PANS—pictures and new services—over fiber-optic cable.

Richard Snelling and other Baby Bell leaders, together with the Bellcore laboratory (the part of Bell Labs assigned to the Baby Bells), compose what is potentially a commanding force in global telecommunications and a major asset of American competitiveness. They are responsible for about 30 percent of high-technology capital spending.

These companies are potential American Goliaths in global competition. But the antitrust courts and Congress have put them in chains. In order to take fiber to the home, for example, Snelling has to persuade the public-utilities commissions in four states that he is not writing off his copper wires too fast in an evil effort to gouge the consumer. He also has to persuade Washington's political establishment that he is not conspiring to overthrow its precious local cable-television monopolies.

In an amazing perversity, the Modified Final Judgment severely restricted the seven Baby Bells from buying equipment from AT&T.

Unless the seven Baby Bells can become cable killers by combining the telephone and television systems, these huge companies will actually weaken U.S. competitiveness. They will continue to channel American capital out of the telecommunications industry and into other investments, such as real estate, financial services, and computer retailing.

Any telecommunications company in the world can operate freely in the U.S. market, manufacturing telephones, television cables, personal computers, facsimile machines, and modems to connect computer equipment to the network—any company, that is, except a Baby Bell. AT&T is a globally competitive manufacturer of many of these products. But in an amazing perversity, showing the blindness of the American legal system to the realities of international competition, the Modified Final Judgment severely restricted the seven Baby Bells from buying equipment from AT&T. To prove that they are not still ensnarled in the old AT&T monopoly, the Bells buy much of their equipment from foreigners. Regulatory pressure poses a triple threat to U.S. competitiveness: it weakens AT&T (America's major producer of telecommunications gear), strengthens foreign manufacturers of this vital teletechnology, and artificially increases the U.S. trade gap.

Even worse for the the regional Bells, any company can lay bypass lines that completely circumvent the Bell system. Tied in knots by regulations, the Baby Bells are forbidden to compete effectively in telecommunications.

In the early 1980s, when the U.S. position in telecommunications was about to collapse, junk bonds and venture capital saved the day by financing MCI and hundreds of new semiconductor firms. Today, the U.S. faces a similar crisis. This time, the solution is to unleash the Baby Bells. The Bells command ample capital to provide the bulk of fiber and the switching systems needed to create a new domonetic environment for American growth.

To achieve this goal, no major new government appropriations are needed. No new protectionist rules are required. Instead, we need a new prison protest movement: Free Richard Snelling and the Bell Seven.

9:58 PM, Memphis, Tennessee. Inventory pulled from our warehouse facility for overnight delivery.

Federal Express PartsBank® provides warehousing and distribution of your products. It's just one of many Business Logistics Services we offer.

THE TELEFUTURE

I first declared the coming death of television and the birth of the telecomputer in two articles published in early 1989 and then in my book *Microcosm*. The death of television, I wrote, would be the salvation of American competitiveness. At the time, I thought that the leaders of U.S. electronic firms would rejoice at the news. I was wrong.

I debated the fate of TV with Richard Elkus Jr., president of Prometrix Corporation and one of the developers of the videotape recorder, at the U.S. Telephone Association convention in San Francisco on the day of the earthquake. I debated it further with Jerry Pearlman, CEO of Zenith, at the Maximum Service Telecasters seminar in Washington, D.C.; with MIT professor Charles Ferguson on the *MacNeil/Lehrer NewsHour*; with several members of the American Electronics Association at an impromptu encounter in the Silicon Valley; and before a U.S. congressional committee. Although a few listeners applauded, most were appalled.

The American Electronics Association said that if Japan prevailed in the manufacture of HDTV, the U.S. electronics industry would face severe decline. At a conference held in Washington, D.C., by *Electronic Engineering Times*, no fewer than seven of the speakers, including two congressmen, devoted their presentations to refuting my arguments. When I discussed my ideas with business and technical leaders from AT&T, Bellcore, Intel, and Tektronix, most of them were deeply skeptical or overtly indignant.

The responses varied from industry to industry, but nearly all the executives shied from the sharp implications for their own businesses. Broadcasters, posing as members of a public utility, nervously told me of the precious benefits of "free and universal" television service. They scoffed at the idea that huge new markets existed for narrowcast programming. TV is a boob tube, the broadcasters implied, because at heart most watchers are boobs.

The cable operators, having run circles around the phone companies throughout the decade, laughed at my idea that they would be usurped by the Baby Bells. Phone service and cable service are very different, they said; there will always be two wires running into the home. If you want fiber, we will provide it in broadcast configurations but not in ISDN standards. You want telecomputers? they asked. Well, John Malone, CEO of Tele-communications Inc. (TCI), is investing heavily in a cable service for personal-computer users. Pushing the issue further posed a personal problem for me, since my brother works for a cable operator. But I did push it, and the cable people, including my brother, merely shrugged; they were entrepreneurs and could handle whatever was coming.

In letters, phone calls, and face-to-face encounters, on-line database executives expressed indignation at my idea that their services were obsolete. They said they were making money hand over fist, and they planned to make a whole lot more. They pointed to the great value of their software and equipment, their rich libraries of valuable information, and their high price-earnings ratios. They denied that their formidable operations could ever be duplicated on a desktop.

When I urged my friends in the computer industry to focus more on the low end of the market, they recalled years of setbacks in earlier efforts to sell computers to the home (before the technology was ready). They cited studies that showed that computers and television sets are now used for completely different purposes in different rooms of the home. Besides, they pointed out triumphantly, TV viewers want a big screen, whereas computer users want a small display.

The U.S. microchip-industry leaders I talked to were not as concerned with beating Japanese consumer products as they were with selling microchips to be used in those products. They pretended that the primary threat from Japan was not manufacturing excellence and marketing ingenuity but "illegal dumping." Telephone executives were nervous if I even brought up the subject of their displacing broadcast cable through fiber optics. Several of them urgently warned me of the overpowering political clout of the cable and broadcasting industries. Jess Chernak, AT&T's leading champion of fiber, pointed out that today only analog transmission through cable can allow "windowing," which enables the viewer to watch several shows on a screen at once. TV watchers won't want to lose that feature, he said. Executives in AT&T's components division chiefly wanted to tell me about the immense opportunities in microchip production for TV sets. Bellcore officials stressed their long-term strategy to take fiber to the home over the next 30 years, carrying mainly voice and computer data.

At a time of drastic upheaval, U.S. firms have adopted a narrow and shortsighted focus.

Most American executives, obsessed with current Japanese plans and products, refused to see that technological change is reshuffling all forms of information-sharing. At a time of drastic upheaval, U.S. firms have adopted a narrow and shortsighted focus. Jerry Pearlman of Zenith is concerned only with making TVs; most telephone executives see their primary role as providing wire channels for voice communications; television broadcasters just want to offer more of the same recipe of news and entertainment through free access to the spectrum; John Malone of TCI seeks to enrich and expand his cable networks in the same outdated broadcasting mode; John Akers of IBM is concentrating mainly on making computers for businesses.

All of these industry leaders will be disappointed with the outcome of their efforts. Jerry Pearlman may think that divesting his company's computer divisions will allow it to concentrate on expanding its television market, but Zenith's market share will grow in the long term only if it starts making computers again. Most broadcasters and cable programmers will have to give up the mass-appeal game and begin focusing on the opportunities arising in narrowcast video programming. The database industry may want to keep control of its data and parcel it out over telephone lines to corporate subscribers, but its survival depends on packaging information for people's desktops and living rooms. The U.S. computer industry will have to understand that the biggest threat to its dominance will come from cheap video super-computers sold for use in the home by Japanese TV manufacturers.

No information company will be exempt from this sweep of industrial transformation. Except for a few special applications, sending voice signals alone through wires or pictures through the air simply will not pay. The air will provide sufficient bandwidth for voice communication over wireless phones or the radio. The air is a hopeless bottleneck, however, for the huge bandwidth needed to transmit images.

As time passes, this bottleneck will become more and more obvious. The spread of mobile-phone technologies will create powerful new competition for the spectrum space now hogged by television. The plummeting price of computer video will create an ever-growing demand for alternative distribution modes for video programming. The limitations of the spectrum, combined with new technology, will dictate a reversal in the proportionate use of wire and air for audio and video. This is the essence of the "telefuture." Voice communication, now conducted through wires, will be carried over the air. Entertainment data, now broadcast over the air, will be transmitted through fiber-optic wires.

Because government regulations deter the Baby Bells from investing in telecommunications, they are diverting their capital into real estate and computer retailing. When these regulatory controls are amended in the future, however, the Bells will have to put every available dollar into preparing their networks for the telefuture. The cable industry, beset on one side by the power of fiber and on the other by the growing efficiency of direct-broadcast satellite, will survive in its present form only if the politicians continue to protect it.

The Japanese have clear goals for their own telefuture. Although their fiber network is now far smaller than America's, the Japanese plan to spend some $120 billion to take fiber to the home by the year 2000. They also plan to spend another $150 billion to create entire "information cities." These cities will be completely wired with digital fiber networks connecting and transforming schools, libraries, hospitals, offices, and all the now-separate analog industries. A large Japanese lead in laying fiber to the home would allow them to wrest leadership from Corning and AT&T, whose fiber production

2:45 PM, Hong Kong. Shipments arriving.

Every business day, Federal Express flies nearly 400,000 miles and drives 1.5 million miles to deliver packages throughout the world.

1:00 PM, Paris, France. Pick-up near Eiffel Tower.

Our international air express delivery network
is already helping business in Western Europe prepare for 1992.

is leveling off as America's long-distance network is being completed.

By producing enough fiber for the homes and offices of Japan, NTT and Sumitomo can achieve volumes of output well above current American levels. According to learning-curve theory, manufacturing costs drop between 20 and 30 percent every time accumulated volume is doubled. This means that the cost of Sumitomo's fiber will drop drastically in relation to American companies' cost. There will be nothing that Corning or AT&T can do about that. Unless the U.S. also installs fiber to the home, Japan's fiber will be so much cheaper that American industries will beg Japan to sell it to them so that they can stay competitive.

Laying fiber to the home, however, will yield gains extending far beyond the fiber industry. By vastly increasing the bandwidth of information channels to the home, Japan will also spur the development of its computer, microchip, and optoelectronics industries. Essential for telecomputer networks, optoelectronics is the technology for joining the light pulses of the fiber network to the electronic pulses of computers. Other advanced microchips are essential to the fast digital video processing needed in all high-definition systems.

U.S. telephone and computer executives, who speak of the year 2010 or even 2030 as the target for completing an American network, are kidding themselves. If the U.S. does not act sooner, the network will be built by Japan and made of Japanese fiber and optoelectronics and possibly Japanese computers. Much of the system used by the U.S. might even be located in Japan. As Jack McDonald, executive vice-president of Contel Corporation, has warned, a Japanese edge in switching efficiency might well mean that calls between San Francisco and Los Angeles will be switched in Tokyo.

Many American executives throw up their hands in despair over the price of a fiber system. Experts estimate that installing an entirely glass phone network would cost between $100 billion and $300 billion. Additional billions would be needed to build high-definition telecomputer screens and new video memories. Where will the money come from? Most electronics-industry lobbyists agree on a solution. The way to finance the wiring of the U.S., they say, is through massive government subsidies and guarantees. But as White House budget officials plaintively point out, there are hundreds of other worthy seekers of such funds, from AIDS researchers and bioengineers to high-energy physicists and space scientists.

Fiber to the home must be financed not through the government but by the U.S. computer and telecommunications industries, which will reap the rewards from this vast commercial undertaking. One obvious source for the funds is

The U.S. regulatory system is holding back industry leaders from competing with Japan in the vast tele- communications market.

the Baby Bells. In 1989, the Bells boasted revenues of more than $70 billion and earned profits of nearly $9 billion. Their earnings have been growing at a pace of about 5 percent a year for the last five years, mostly from phone service alone. Any accelerated program for fiber to the home, though, would have to include entertainment video to make it pay. The U.S. cable operators could contribute; they command a cash flow of several billion dollars a year. Under deregulation, other possible contributors to the network would include the long-distance carriers, from AT&T to GTE; the electric utilities that string glass wires within their electric cables; and other companies, like Williams Telecommunications Group, that want to share in the technology. American industry, released from its regulatory shackles, could finance a program of fiber to the home without any government aid.

Japanese TV manufacturers clearly aim for a step-by-step conversion of their outmoded box into a powerful computer.

Most U.S. business and political leaders, however, are ignoring this possibility. They see the struggle for the tele-future as a contest between the U.S. and Japan in the con-sumer-electronics market. They focus on television even though the U.S. commands the computer industry, which uses the most rapidly-advancing technology in the history of mankind. Japanese TV manufacturers understand this weakness in the American vision. They clearly aim for a step-by-step conversion of their outmoded box into a powerful computer. They know that the country that can first converge the worlds of information and entertainment will become the global computer and telecommunications leader.

American companies not only largely rule the global com-puter business, with a worldwide market share of nearly 70 percent, but the U.S. is unchallenged in the critical arenas of entrepreneurial creativity. While the TV-set industry consists mostly of a few gigantic Asian and European conglomerates, the computer business in the U.S. is composed of some 20,000 firms, including 14,000 software companies. Nearly 800 digital image-processing companies are devoted directly to the technologies of telecomputing, along with nearly 1,000 firms in the field of multimedia programming. The U.S., however, doesn't seem to realize that it already commands the technologies it needs for developing the telecomputer.

By extending the life of television into the next century with HDTV, the Japanese hope to thwart the age of the telecomputer until they can rule it.

The telecomputer is on its way. One of the most ambitious telecomputer concepts, launched by veterans of Next and Apple, goes by the name of Frox. This machine will connect with CD-ROMs, edit out television advertisements, program the VCR, search databases for selected news items, and—significantly—answer the telephone. When America installs fiber to the home, Frox and the many other machines now being launched by Intel Corporation and small companies such as Mass Microsystems and Aapps Inc., can become fully digitized and tap new worlds of interactive video information.

While executives in major American electronics firms concentrate on all the reasons a telecomputer strategy will fail, entrepreneurs in literally thousands of other U.S. companies are showing how it will succeed. Any visitor to the 1989 Siggraph, Comdex, Macworld, Multimedia, or Hypermedia conventions, with their exhibits of new technology, could sense the onrush of American computer video, graphics, and networking creativity.

The Japanese fully understand the strategic importance of computer technology and software to the future of information-sharing. In 1988, the world's VCR manufacturers made $3 billion in revenues from the sale of videocassette recorders to the U.S. During the same period, U.S. film studios made $4.5 billion in revenues from selling videocassette films. In 1989, Sony spent $3.4 billion for Columbia Pictures, or 350 times the studio's annual earnings, and then paid $700 million for the rights to the services of Hollywood executives Peter Guber and Jon Peters, the producers of *Batman*. The Japanese are learning that although the microchip makes high-quality digital video possible, software makes it usable—and valuable.

In the face of the American threat, the Japanese plan to use their strength in television to help gain the time and technology that would eventually allow them to take the lead in the computer industry. By extending the life of television into the next century with HDTV, the Japanese hope to thwart the age of the telecomputer until they can rule it. The American establishment is being sidetracked by this Japanese strategy. Even AT&T, which should be the technological spearhead of

the move to the telecomputer, has formed an alliance with Zenith, the last American-owned television producer, to revive American top-down broadcasting through HDTV.

All the fiefdoms of the television age must give way to the new imperative of the computer age: the creation of a national integrated services digital network of fiber optics. Launching an era of true telecomputing, this technology would not only make the U.S. a major force in consumer electronics but would also help the nation address its critical problems of culture and education.

T he key to advancing this technology is the creation of a sound industrial policy—one that focuses not on regulations that promote U.S. television production but on the removal of government obstacles to the rapid deployment of fiber optics. Four measures will be required to unleash the Baby Bells into the business of entertainment video—a crucial step toward paying for fiber to the home. The FCC must relax its 1970 restrictions on cross-ownership of cable and telephone lines so that the phone companies can transmit video entertainment throughout their own regions. Judge Greene must relax the restrictions in his Modified Final Judgment so that the phone companies can enter information-based businesses, including transmission of TV programs. Congress must revise the 1984 Cable Communications Policy Act to end the entertainment-video cable monopolies. It must also abolish the powers of state public-utilities commissions to regulate Bell investments. All of these measures must add up to a resolute decision to deregulate American telecommunications.

Unlike the drive for HDTV, a campaign to promote fiber optics would be simple and practical. It would be a sure winner. It would use U.S. technology, U.S. workers, and U.S. corporations. By creating a new network of fiber to the home, the telephone companies could revitalize the American information economy and regain their central role in telecommunications.

The new laws of domonetics are hostile to hierarchies, monopolies, industrial bureaucracies, and other top-down systems of all kinds. Just as intelligence and control are moving from gigantic mainframes to personal computers, from centralized databases to desktop libraries, from the central Bell pyramid to a new array of communications tools, and from a few national broadcast networks to millions of programmers around the globe, so is economic power shifting from mass institutions to individuals.

Industrially, technologically, and politically, these trends are playing to America's strengths. They offer an exhilarating opportunity to enlarge freedom, to revitalize culture, and to prosper.

In the air and on the ground, Federal Express is
working to meet the needs of business throughout the world.

Additional Copies

To order additional copies of *Life After Television*
for friends or colleagues, please write to
The Larger Agenda Series, Whittle Direct Books,
505 Market St., Knoxville, Tenn. 37902.
Please include the recipient's name, mailing
address, and, where applicable, title, company
name, and type of business.

For a single copy, please enclose a check for $11.95
payable to The Larger Agenda Series. When
ordering 10 or more books, enclose $9.95 for
each; for orders of 50 or more books, enclose
$7.95 for each. If you wish to place an order by
phone, call 800-284-1956.

Also available, at the same prices, are copies
of the previous books in The Larger Agenda Series:
The Trouble With Money by William Greider,
and *Adhocracy: The Power to Change*
by Robert H. Waterman Jr.

Please allow two weeks for delivery.
Tennessee residents must add 7¾ percent sales tax.